HURT 2 HOPE

HURT 2 HOPE

Heal the Pain of Loss, Grief, and Adversity

Betsy Guerra, PhD

Edited by Susan Ford Collins, Sarah Cherres, and Caroline de Posada

Copyright © Betzaida E. Guerra, PhD, PA

All rights reserved. No part of this publication may be reproduced, distributed, or transmitted in any form or by any means, including photocopying, recording, or other electronic or mechanical methods, without the prior written permission of the publisher, except in the case of brief quotations embodied in critical reviews and certain other noncommercial uses permitted by copyright law. For permission requests, write to the author at the website below.

This publication is meant as a source of valuable information for the reader, however it is not meant as a substitute for direct expert assistance. If such level of assistance is required, the services of a competent professional should be sought.

The names and identifying details of some people in the book have been changed.

ISBN 978-1-7361290-0-5
Library of Congress Control Number: 2020922503

Edited by Susan Ford Collins, Sarah Cherres, and Caroline de Posada

Cover by Erica Giner, Jessika Soto, and McKenna Martinez

Photography by Hazel Rodriguez

First printing edition 2020

Published by
Betzaida E. Guerra, PhD, PA
Miami, FL

To my children.

Fofi, you gave me the gift of life by giving up your own. Accept this book as my tribute to you. It is also an attempt to keep your memory alive by sharing your legacy of love with the world.

Chichi, Gordi, Mia, you gave me the strength to carry on when I felt like giving up on life. You are my greatest source of joy and inspiration. Receive these words as an embrace from your sister in Heaven. May you find hope and comfort in them, especially when Mami is no longer here to whisper them in your ears.

To my husband.

You are my love, my partner, my life. This is our story, and only because you love me, I have been able to transform a tragedy into a fairytale. I love you beyond measure.

Contents

Foreword..vii
Introduction..x

Part One: Hurt

Chapter One	August 25, 2013	1
Chapter Two	Rock Bottom	15
Chapter Three	Slipping Into Darness	23
Chapter Four	Life After Death	29
Chapter Five	Celebration of Life	37
Chapter Six	Healing Begins	51
Chapter Seven	The Birth of A Rainbow	57
Chapter Eight	The Day-to-Day	67
Chapter Nine	Thanks-giving	75
Chapter Ten	Fofi's Third Birthday	89
Chapter Eleven	Surviving The Holidays	99
Chapter Twelve	A New Year	105
Chapter Thirteen	The First Anniversary	123

CONTENTS

Part Two: Hope

Chapter Fourteen	Before We Begin	137
Chapter Fifteen	Five Pillars of Healing	139
Chapter Sixteen	Fertilizing Pain	143
Chapter Seventeen	Acceptance	157
Chapter Eighteen	Interpretation	167
Chapter Nineteen	Team	179
Chapter Twenty	Habits	193
Chapter Twenty-one	Spirituality	219
Chapter Twenty-two	GPS	237
Chapter Twenty-three	Purpose	261
Chapter Twenty-four	Hope	271

Acknowledgments..277

About The Author..283

Foreword

I'll never forget that phone call. I'd put the boys to bed and was lying in bed, reading. My cell phone vibrated. It was my friend, Lisie, who rarely calls. I found it odd she was calling at that time.

"Hey, girl" I answered cheerfully.

"Caro. Have you heard?"

"What's going on?"

"There's been an accident. Alain and Betsy's daughter. They were in the pool…"

I sat up, grabbing my husband's arm. "Hold on, wait, which daughter? Is she okay? Tell me she's okay?"

Lisie's voice cracked. "No, Caro. It's not okay. It's Fofi. She didn't make it."

Orlando leaned in to grasp what was happening. I wailed. "Where are they?" I asked. "At the hospital." Lisie offered to come and stay with my kids so I could be with my friends.

Orlando jumped out of bed and rushed to put on a pair of jeans and a shirt.

"This can't be happening; this can't be happening." We cried all the way to the hospital. I thought Lisie was wrong. I hoped to get to the hospital and discover they had saved

FOREWORD

her. But all we found was a large gathering of friends and family with nothing but sadness and despair in their eyes.

Fofi's passing affected me deeply. I had never truly known empathy until I mourned Alain and Betsy's loss as if it were my own. But no matter how devastated I felt, I knew it paled in comparison to what they were going through. I often wondered if they could ever overcome a tragedy like this one.

What I saw happen next was life-altering. I witnessed this couple find their way to happiness again after going through the unimaginable.

Betsy has always prided herself on being a woman who walks the talk. Being in a profession that counsels people for a living, she didn't want to just tell people how to live their lives, save their marriages, and overcome grief. She wanted to exemplify the principles she taught.

Well, I have seen her do the work firsthand, and I am amazed and inspired by her courage and resilience.

When Betsy set out to write this book, I knew it wouldn't be easy. She'd already been through this heart-wrenching journey and finally gotten to a good place — and I knew this book would force her to relive those difficult moments.

But she did it anyway.

FOREWORD

She did it for her daughter—to honor her life and her legacy; and she did it for you—to give you hope and the tools to find happiness again.

As you read this book, I want you to know that Betsy has done the work for the last seven years. She has put the tools she teaches in this book into practice. She has sat in her pain, claimed her FAITH, and has chosen to be happy again.

Even though this book didn't come easy to her, she labored through it because she knew you needed it.

Betsy, her family, and this book are beacons of hope for all of us.

Caroline de Posada, Author of Looking Over the Edge

Introduction

Make her heart beat! Make her heart beat! Make her heart beat!

I begged God to save my daughter while I stared helplessly at the hospital monitor.

My life changed that day.

My smile became a frown. My dreams turned into nightmares. My hope vanished. All I could feel was deep sorrow.

I know Pain.

I've experienced it in the day to day when things don't go my way, and I have lived it in the excruciating agony of losing a loved one.

My career as a psychotherapist furthered my exposure to suffering. I learned that I could connect with my clients' pain, regardless of the cause, because they were suffering loss too.

We think we only grieve when a person dies, but the truth is we mourn for many reasons. We endure the loss of time, youth, health, relationships, dreams, and expectations. We also lose money, freedom, respect, confidence, peace, and people. Any time we lose our life as we knew it, we grieve.

The pain of loss unites us, but it is our response to it that defines us.

INTRODUCTION

Having gone through the unimaginable, I had the opportunity to use my clinical expertise and spiritual background for my own healing. I learned firsthand how to go from deep hurt to grand hope, and I am devoted to helping you do the same.

In this book, I will teach you how to use your pain to rise above adversity and find your way to joy. In Part One, I share my personal story. I wrote this section in tears, so fear not if you feel vulnerable as you read it. Sitting with your ache is the beginning of healing.

In Part Two, I lead you to hope. I empower you with tools that will increase your strength throughout this process. I also show you how to tap into your inner wisdom, so that you may live in peace and with purpose. In this section, I share stories of clients whose names I've changed to protect their identity.

I wrote these words with an open heart and beg you to read them with the same disposition. Please know that I can't talk about my life sincerely without mentioning God. I am a woman of faith. I tried to honor your different beliefs by using terms such as *higher power*, *divine*, and *Source*, but to stay true to myself, I couldn't omit my heavenly Father. I respect each of your spiritual values and humbly ask that you make mental substitutions for whatever doesn't resonate with you.

This book is for you if you are hurting, feeling stuck, or simply want to become a better version of yourself. It is a great resource if

INTRODUCTION

you want to support someone you love through hardship or loss. It's also a nice read if you're up for a beautiful true story.

This book, like life itself, is a journey from hurt to hope.

Betsy Guerra, PhD

HURT 2 HOPE

Part One: Hurt

CHAPTER 1

August 25, 2013

It must have been shortly after seven in the morning when the hallway door flung open, revealing my precious 2-year-old with her crazed and curly brown hair. She smiled with her entire face, as she usually did, causing me to smile back. "Good morning, princess," I said joyfully as I kneeled and opened up my arms to welcome her. She rushed to my embrace, where I held and covered her up with kisses.

Daddy was cooking breakfast, and he called Fofi over for their morning guessing game. He gave her a freshly pressed juice, and she had to guess what it was made of. "Oranges and apples," she said confidently with a smirk on her face and her curious big brown eyes. "Yes!" Daddy exclaimed, tickling her as she giggled.

Her siblings, 4-year-old Chichi and 1-year-old Gordi, woke up shortly after to the same warm welcome. After breakfast, we got ready to attend the 9:30 a.m. Sunday Mass. We walked into the church, and I contemplated Fofi's beautiful dress swaying to the rhythm of her "bouncy" walk.

When it was time to recite the *Our Father* prayer in the Mass, Fofi was excited to show off what she had been learning every night. I was teaching her the English version of that prayer because she already knew it in Spanish, her first language. Her English version was extra special because she recited it with an adorable accent. She looked up at the sweet old lady standing next to her and finished her sentences just as she did it at bedtime:

"Our...".

"Fatha.."

"who art in..."

"Heaven..."

"Hallowed be thy..."

"Nay..."

It was so beautiful! Her innocence and holiness moved me. I was raising her for God. I felt at that moment that my efforts were paying off.

After Mass, I watched her "go in peace" holding the hand of our family friend, Rina, who took her to greet our Blessed Mother. The image of Mary stood just a few steps away, facing me. I remember the sun shining over the colorful glass adorning the back wall of the sculpture. The rays created a rainbow surrounding the silhouettes of my little princess and her big friend. While still holding hands, they both looked up and contemplated Mary. I smiled as I watched from afar, taking in the beauty of that simple—yet profound—moment. Before walking away, Rina lifted Fofi up so she could kiss the hand of her heavenly Mom.

We drove home after Mass, ready to enjoy the last pool day of the summer. I stayed inside the house breastfeeding Gordi, Fofi's baby brother, while she and her big sister, Chichi, went to Home Depot with my husband, Alain. The girls wanted to help Daddy pick a new grill for our outdoor family day. I put my son down for a nap and served the girls lunch when they returned from the store. They ate outside at the picnic table by the pool. Then, they played in the backyard with my husband. I went back to the kitchen to pick up and get ready for our guests.

As people started to arrive, Fofi went inside the house to get me. She said, "Mami, yo quiero estar donde tú estés," which translates to, "Mommy, I want to be where you are..." That was her way of asking me to go into the pool with her. Fortunately, I did.

We called my husband, Alain, from the pool to join our usual cheerleading game. I carried Fofi on my shoulders, and Daddy carried us on his. Her little but strong hands clutched my head. I imagined it was her way of feeling safe.

Although she enjoyed the pool and the beach tremendously, she was very cautious. I attributed her wariness to the "survival" classes I enrolled her in when we moved into the house a year prior.

I've always thought the lessons traumatized her because they forced her to do things she was afraid of, like being thrown underwater without first feeling safe.

I still remember her shivering. I never knew whether she was cold or scared. "It's normal. It'll get better after a couple of days," the instructor reassured me. But it never did. I feel guilty now about having trusted a stranger more than my intuition as a mother. At the time, I figured half an hour of crying daily for one week would lead to a lifetime of water safety.

After the first cheerleading pose, my oldest daughter, Chichi, joined us. I put Fofi on one of my shoulders and her big sister on the other. Daddy picked us up and placed the three of us on his shoulders. Chichi gave Fofi confidence, so this time she threw her hands up in the air during her cheer performance. Chichi was an amazing big sister, and they were the best of friends. They were so close that it was hard to imagine one without the other.

At the end of the game, Fofi showed off everything she had been learning at her new swim school. We registered her shortly after the survival classes to help her feel safe and regain confidence. Her instructor taught Fofi to love swimming and helped her taper her fear.

That summer day, she moved past her fear. She was so excited about her swimming abilities that she'd ask us to watch her swim from Daddy to me, back and forth. We were so proud!

The moment took me back to memories of the previous weekend. We were in Puerto Rico for my parents' 40th anniversary. We spent one day at the Ritz Carlton in Isla Verde, where we enjoyed the pool.

Fofi was playing in the steps at the shallow end with me. Then, she grabbed onto the handrail, like a monkey, with both her hands and feet. I loved that she was always so active and adventurous. She was the perfect balance between a girlie girl and a tomboy. One minute she would play dress-up with her sister, and the next, she would roll in the grass, barefoot, with her little brother.

After hanging from the rails for a few seconds, she let go of her feet but didn't have enough momentum to shift her body upright and feel the steps. Fofi began whining and anxiously crying out for help. I couldn't understand why she was so afraid when I was right by her. Fear is an alert meant to keep us safe from dangerous situations. It comforted me to know that Fofi was scared of water when she was not yet a skilled swimmer. She used to stay in the shallow end and refrained from submerging herself in the pool without adult supervision. But now she was a better swimmer, and her fear prevented her from enjoying the water. It was important for me to model the distinction between fear as a safety mechanism versus fear as a habit.

That day at the Ritz, I used the opportunity to reassure Fofi. I grabbed her, and she wrapped her little legs around my waist. "Sweetie do not be afraid. Mommy will take care of you."

A short week later, Fofi was no longer scared of swimming. She was fearless that sunny Miami afternoon at our pool.

We had over 30 guests witnessing our brave girl's swimming abilities. There were about ten adults in their thirties chatting in the pool, while seven of our young children played with water toys along the side. Other friends and family members gathered around the pool area. The grandparents stayed cool inside the house, watching us have fun through the window.

The men of the family were by the tiki hut just a few feet away from the pool. They were hanging out with my husband while he put steaks and burgers on the brand new grill he bought with our daughters that morning. Everyone was enjoying the warmth of our new home and family.

It was a perfect day.

Until the clock struck five.

I was standing in the pool chatting with my friend, Cristi. Suddenly, she asked, "Where's Fofi?"

She had just been playing with the other kids. She had been right by me. What caused Cristi to ask for Fofi? Something about her question shot fear into my heart. I became panic-stricken in a split second like my Fofi felt at the Ritz the week prior.

I scanned the area at lightning speed.

Where is she?

My chest tightened.

My heart pounded.

I still couldn't find her anywhere. I zoomed in with hypervigilant eyes.

She was right by me.

My gaze shifted down.

She was beside me…but at the bottom.

There, through the clear and blurry water, I caught a glimpse of my daughter's red and white polka-dot Minnie Mouse bathing suit.

At the bottom of that traitor body of water lay my precious two-year-old daughter, Fofi.

Immediately, I dove in to grab her. I held my breath as I clutched her body in my arms to rush her to the surface. I struggled to pull us both above the water, pushing against the resistance that tried to keep us down.

I managed to carry her out of the water and laid her on the pavers by the edge of the pool. Foamy water started coming out from her nose or mouth. It is hard to remember.

I think I screamed for help. I tried to give her CPR, but I wasn't sure I knew what I was doing. Although there was commotion and hysteria in the background, for me the world stopped. It was just the two of us.

My husband rushed to our side. His eyes revealed the fear I felt when I heard Cristi's question. Instinctively, we knew how terrible this was.

He spoke to her as though there was no one else around. "You are strong, my love," he said with a tone of hopeful desperation while holding her lifeless body in his arms. "Stay with me. You can do this. Look at Daddy," he commanded as he moved her shoulders, trying to get a reaction from her. He spoke to her, kissed her, and repeatedly brought her face toward his heart in an embrace.

I experienced what happened next as if I were watching my life unravel in a movie. I silently wailed in desperation, witnessing each second pass in slow motion. My thoughts repeated over and over this is not happening this can't be true.

Someone called 911 and put the phone to my ear. I managed to dictate my home address to the emergency operator. I then handed the cell phone over to one of my guests, who was a physician at Baptist Hospital.

"She has a pulse," Jannelle responded to the 911 operator.

Her presence gave me hope.

"Save her, my friend. Please save her!" I begged.

Janelle didn't look up at me. She couldn't. She was no longer my friend she was the doctor. The responsibility of saving my daughter's life consumed her. She seemed terrified.

Alain held our little girl while Janelle examined her. I knew he wouldn't leave Fofi's side. I felt compelled to pray.

I am a woman of faith. I believe in a God of love and mercy that I knew would save my daughter, and I couldn't waste a minute on fear. Please save her, my dear Lord. Save my little girl. I made big promises in exchange for His mercy. I felt peace amidst the terror because I was so sure He would listen to my supplication.

My neighbor approached me as I paced back and forth near our kids' trampoline. "Have faith, my love," Gladys whispered as she hugged me.

"I know that God will save her," I responded confidently. Gladys squeezed me tighter and then gave me the space to turn around and continue praying alone. Please save her, Dear God. I'm raising her for you. Let me finish my job. Please save my little girl.

Gladys was a woman in her 60s. She was the only one that built up the courage to come close and console me. Everyone else's shock kept them spectating from a distance.

Gladys was so full of love and tenderness that I couldn't help but see her as a motherly figure. She was my angel when she embraced me then and continues to be so today from heaven. As I wrote this book, she battled pancreatic cancer. She fought like the warrior she was, and I truly believe her grit and joyful attitude bought her a few more years of life. She still died before I was ready to lose her.

Minutes later, the paramedics arrived. They worked on my sleeping beauty and moved her unresponsive body to the ambulance. Someone brought me dry clothes to put on over my wet bathing suit, and I pulled them on hurriedly.

I still remember the chilling air that pierced through my bones as we sat in the front seat of that air-conditioned ambulance. My entire body was shaking. Alain noticed and embraced me to help contain the shivering. The ambulance driver was kind and reassuring, though I don't remember his face or his words. Everything was a blur, including the siren that was blaring in the background—or so it seemed. It must have been just above us.

How many times do we hear an ambulance as we walk or drive, failing to realize that it could be the sound of death for someone? The siren sound haunted me for months. I heard ambulances often as they rushed down 87th Avenue, near my home.

Within five minutes, we arrived at Baptist Hospital. They took us to the emergency room immediately. The room felt small and crowded by the medical staff taking care of our little girl. The doctors spoke in quick commands and responses, like my friend Janelle had done earlier. Their focus was on her. I could see how much they cared about Fofi. I trusted them.

Be her doctor, Dear God. Save her through them, I prayed. *Give them the wisdom to do whatever is needed. Please save her!*

The doctors tried urgently to save her. I can't recall the details because the moment was chaotic and surreal. The only thing real was the pain. I can still feel it as I revisit the scene to write these words for you.

There was a monitor to the right side of her stretcher where my husband and I stood. I didn't know how to interpret the data it showed, but I did notice a straight line. Was that *the* flat line?

Make her heart beat! Make her heart beat! Make her heart beat! I begged God with unwavering faith. I've always felt that we need to be specific when we pray, and that's what I did at that moment, to the best of my abilities.

My brain was drained and paralyzed, but it felt too risky to stop praying. I had to let God know that I believed. I asked Him to give me a phrase or scripture I could repeat in prayer without having to think.

I can do all things through Christ who strengthens me... (Philippians 4:13)

No! I rejected that scripture because it suggested that Fofi wouldn't make it. I figured it was my fear and hopelessness bringing it to me. I knew God would save her. He had to! He loved me and He knew I loved Him. *Be her doctor, dear God. Save my little girl. Make her heart beat.*

Suddenly, amidst the turmoil, I heard an inner voice say, "You know Fofi could be saved and not be the Fofi you knew."

I thought about my oldest sister who was born healthy but suffered from rubella when she was nine months old. The high fever from the disease created complications and put her in a coma. She almost died, but *God made her heart beat.*

Even though my sister survived, my parents' dreams for her didn't. She suffered neurological impairments that caused severe mental retardation, epilepsy, and an inability to speak or be independent. Enormous pain came from the challenges her condition created, but her life was still a gift. "She's a blessing from God," my parents would say repeatedly. My sister was my family's miracle, but she was no longer the girl my parents once knew.

The inner voice continued, what if He made her heart beat, but she stopped being the sweet, jolly, funny girl we knew? What if her heart beats, but her brain dies? What if…?

My mind was quick to react. I don't care! She's my daughter. I'll love her regardless. Let her heart beat, God. Please don't take her. Make her heart beat!

Minutes that seemed eternal, yet not long enough, passed by. The medical staff continued fighting for her life. My husband positioned himself closer to her peaceful face and said, "Come on, Fofi. You are strong. Wake up. We're going to watch a movie tonight. You've got this!"

My heart was crushed. I'm not sure which pain was more excruciating—the one that came from the possibility of losing my daughter or the one caused by witnessing my husband's pain and desperation. I was powerless. I couldn't do anything to save my Fofi's life, nor could I mend the pieces of Alain's broken heart.

All I could do was pray…so I did. Incessantly. *Save my Fofi, dear Lord. Make her heart beat. Be her doctor. Use the medical staff as your vessel. Show them the way to bring my princess to life.* I repeated my prayers over and over again. Then I added, reluctantly, *let your will be done.*

Suddenly my prayer became a song. I didn't plan for it, and I don't know how it happened. I just know that my knees buckled, and I found myself kneeling by the stretcher, singing *Cántico Celeste* (Heavenly Chant). It was a song of hope that I often sang for my girls as a lullaby. Its lyrics reassured me that the night and its dread would pass and that soon the sun would light up my heart.

At that moment, I knew God's will was different than mine. The pain was so unbearable, I disconnected from my senses. I left my body as I did by the pool moments earlier. The movie I didn't want to watch continued to unfold before me.

Everything was happening fast and in slow motion. The loud turmoil was mute. I knew they were talking, but I couldn't understand what the medical staff was saying. It was all a blur, except when I looked at my husband.

The only thing I could see clearly was that Alain still had hope. He paid attention to every move the doctors made and he spoke to our sleeping Fofi with endearing, encouraging words. Then, he turned to me and said, "Fofi is strong. They're trying something new. This will work."

I'm the optimist in our relationship; the dreamer, the believer, the last one to lose hope. Alain is by no means a pessimist, but he likes to call himself a "realist." He is the skeptical, rational, and logical one. Together we are amazing. He brings me back to Earth when I need to be practical, and I sprinkle dreams into his life when reality doesn't seem promising.

This time, it was my husband's optimism that brought me back to my senses. His unwavering faith and hope, in this moment, only made my pain stronger. It's one thing to endure your own heartache, but it's far more agonizing to witness the pain of the person you love most in this world. I could feel the ache as it consumed every bone in my body, one at a time.

The faces of the medical staff said what we were not ready to hear. Their droopy, sad eyes and disheartened spirits conveyed that there was nothing else they could do. They must have said, "I'm sorry," or something like that. I watched as, one by one, they lowered their gaze to the floor and slowly left the room.

The monitor still showed a straight line. *The* flat line. God didn't make my daughter's heart beat.

CHAPTER 2

Rock Bottom

I felt my heart flat-lining as the medical staff exited the room in slow motion, leaving my daughter's lifeless body behind. I wanted to scream, but I had no voice. I wanted to wake up, but I was not sleeping. I wanted to die, but my heart kept beating.

It was surreal.

The pain I felt was numbed by disbelief. My thoughts raced. *This can't be happening. How will I live without her? I can't do this. I want to die too. Take me with you, Fofi. How am I going to tell your older sister that she'll never see her best friend again? God, take me too!*

I fell out of touch with my senses once again. It was as if I could see myself from afar. My body was on autopilot. I was breathing because my subconscious made me. I stood because my legs were in the habit of doing so. My body was just there.

We spent the last moments with our daughter's body at the hospital, while friends and family waited outside. My husband's family came into the room to be with us. They cried in disbelief as they took one last look at Fofi's angelic face. Their emotions made everything more real for me. *This is really happening*, I thought to myself, terrified.

I just stood there, witnessing my in-law parents and siblings saying their final goodbyes to our daughter. They touched her, held her hands, caressed her soft curls, and kissed her tender cheeks. I waited for her to open her big, brown eyes or smile in response to their affection. She never did.

I asked for a phone to call my parents. They were in Puerto Rico visiting. My dad answered.

Crying, and with a trembling voice, I managed to say, "Papi, something horrific happened…" I felt his panic.

"What happened?" he asked.

"Papi, Fofi died in the pool," I replied.

My poor dad. I had never heard him lose his composure that way. He started ranting about how he always hated that pool; that we should fill it in with cement.

"Please stop," I said.

I could not listen anymore. I felt him wanting to slip through one of the holes in the phone speaker to be there with me and with *her*. Fofi was his girl. She was equally obsessed with both of her grandfathers and they were crazy about her too.

A God-fearing man, my father believes so wholeheartedly in eternity that he typically doesn't grieve when someone dies because he's focused on the glory the deceased is experiencing.

That was the first time in my life that I saw him feel the pain of loss. It broke my heart to hear him so disarmed but, if I'm completely honest, a part of me treasured his reaction. It made him seem human and made me feel validated, something I typically didn't get from this rational and practical man.

I don't remember talking to my Mom, but I know she was next to Dad. I couldn't speak anymore. I wished they were closer. I wanted so badly to see my parents and my brothers. I needed their warmth.

Only a few more people were allowed to come in. Papucho was one of them. I had fallen in love with this old Cuban man and his wife after spending a weekend with him on a retreat he led. We became so close that I asked if they would officially adopt me as a granddaughter, which they agreed to. Seeing him there soothed my aching heart.

My best friends, Zuly and Vale, also came in. They were at my house during the day, but had already left when everything happened. Their presence filled the void formed by the thousands of miles that separated me from my family.

Someone from the medical staff stepped in to alert us that it was time to say goodbye to Fofi. *He wanted me to leave my daughter? How could I go home without her? What was going on? I couldn't understand what was happening. I felt so lost. This can't be happening! This can't be!* My brain screamed in silence.

My husband and I wanted to be there until the last second. I knew all too well that the body lying on the stretcher was just the shell of my precious daughter, but that was the very flesh I had embraced, caressed, bathed, and held daily for two years, eight months, and 19 days. That was the body I gave birth to and loved into existence. Through her very eyes, I had seen rays of light and joy. Through those lips, I had witnessed countless smiles and felt a thousand kisses. The little hands that laid still now had once held mine or surrounded my neck in a hug.

It was *all* dead…her body, her kisses, her smiles, her hugs…they were all gone.

My life, as I knew it, ended that day. My family was crushed. My dreams were shattered. Everything that Alain and I imagined for our beloved Fofi was destroyed, and so was our hope.

Eventually, everyone exited the room until only Alain and I were left. Realizing that our time with her was running out, he asked me to leave him alone with her for a few minutes. Noticing I could barely hold myself up, Zuly and Vale stood next to me, one each side, and put my arms around them. I couldn't feel my legs on the floor. They literally carried me to the bathroom. I remember moving very slowly, like a car when gas is running out. I had no energy. The freezing cold room was consuming whatever reserve I had left. My clothes were still wet. I shivered in the bathroom. My friends assisted me.

I was in a daze. I felt dead.

When I came back, Alain told me he had shared with Fofi everything he would have said to her on her life milestones: birthdays, First Communion, graduations, quinceañera, and on her wedding day. I couldn't believe it had occurred to him to do this during such a crisis, but I was grateful it did. This warmed my aching heart. I've had many regrets since that day about things I wish I'd done differently but didn't think about then. I've even daydreamed about saving one of her curls, to have a part of her that I could touch and feel when I long for her tender embrace.

All I have left of her now are memories.

It was past 9 pm when we were asked to leave the hospital *without* our daughter.

How was that possible? How could I leave her behind? My little girl was alone! Leaving her felt like I was abandoning her. It was unreal. I was still in disbelief of what was happening.

My body felt heavy as I directed it towards the exit. The doors slid open in anticipation of my departure. Alain's arm around me kept my knees from giving in. His embrace held me up when my entire being wanted to collapse.

As the doors closed behind us, I noticed a multitude of familiar faces. There must have been close to 100 people who went to support us, hoping their joint prayers would result in a miracle.

But the miracle didn't take place that night.

I looked down, not wanting to make eye contact with anyone whose facial expression would reaffirm that this was actually happening. I didn't want to see my pain reflected in others' faces. I felt the urge to escape. If only I could close my eyes and pretend none of it was real!

I don't remember how we got home. My husband says that a police officer drove us, wanting to protect us from newscasters who were surrounding our home. I was afraid of being attacked and questioned by the press as I had seen on TV. I didn't want to speak to anyone. I felt vulnerable and fearful. What was there for me to say? How could people show no mercy for the sake of breaking news?

I just wanted to be safe at home where my other two children were sleeping peacefully, oblivious to the fact that their lives had been changed forever.

To avoid the press, the officer took an alternate route. He pulled his car in through the fence, to the right of our house, and into our backyard. I felt safe and grateful for his kindness.

We walked past the very scene where it had all taken place. The tiki where Alain had barbecued, the pool that had stolen my daughter's life, the windows that revealed our family's terrified faces, and the pavers her body rested on when I lifted her out of the water. Now everything looked serene. There was no sign of terror. There was no one around. The loudest sound was silence.

I walked in through the family room where our friends, Cristi and Gus, waited. They offered to stay with Chichi and Gordi so that my in-laws could join us at the hospital. I realized then that I had no idea where they had been all along. *Did they witness everything?* I worried. I felt guilty for not protecting them but was comforted when I heard my mother-in-law had taken them inside as soon as the commotion started.

I was desperate to see my surviving children. Cristi reassured me and confirmed that both kids were peacefully sleeping. She also mentioned that she gave Gordi yogurt because she couldn't find his milk. He was almost one, and I was still breastfeeding him. As soon as I heard her say this, I became aware of the engorgement in my breasts—reminding me that his feeding was long overdue.

I walked into Gordi's dark room. After removing my still wet shirt, I couldn't resist lifting his chubby body out of his crib and into my arms. I felt his breath on my skin and was relieved by it. I sat down on the glider and held him close to my naked heart. I wanted to experience life at that moment of death. The scent of my body compelled my son to search for milk. I was numb, but I could feel him sucking. He helped me remember that I was still alive.

While breastfeeding Gordi, I found myself having random thoughts: *Is the flavor of my milk different now? Can he taste my pain? Can I pass on the antibodies to spare him from this suffering?*

I also thought about how, *e*ven though I was going through this, I still had to feed my children and attend to their needs. How was I going to care for others when I could barely hold myself up?

Despite my intrusive thoughts, breastfeeding Gordi was grounding. That moment was beautiful. I embraced my son with profound love and, for a second, I imagined that I was hugging Fofi one last time.

CHAPTER 3

Slipping Into Darkness

Mentally drained and physically exhausted, I needed to sleep. Alain consoled me with a hug, giving me enough energy to head to the kitchen to grab a glass of water. On my way, I noticed my brother-in-law bundled up in blankets on our couch. Avian had invited himself to spend the night and assured us he would keep the press away so we could rest peacefully.

The newscasters settled for interviewing the neighbors that night. However, Avian did keep another visitor from intruding. A representative from the Department of Children and Families came by late that night to question us about the accident. She had already asked the neighbors about our parenting style.

The thought of being questioned as a criminal or as a neglectful parent was jarring. *How could anyone think I would hurt my daughter?* "It is standard protocol...," I heard the lady say the next day when she finally got a hold of me. I was grateful for Avian's guarding us that night. I don't think I could've handled "procedure" at that moment.

It must have been after 11pm when I finally dragged my legs toward the same hallway door that Fofi had come through that morning. Alain and I walked together past our master bedroom to the end of the hallway. We decided to sleep with Chichi, in the room she had shared with her beloved sister.

We made it to Fofi's door and her absence hit us like a gust of icy wind. Tears slid down our cheeks. The room was silent, except for the numbing white noise from the air purifier. I wanted to sense Chichi's aliveness the way I had felt Gordi's. To not wake her, I slid quietly into her bed, caressed her hair, and kissed her cheeks. I savored her scent, listened to her breathing, and felt her warmth. Gazing at her tender face with profound love, I took her in with all my senses. I was so grateful she was alive.

But her sister's bed was empty. I couldn't understand how Fofi could have been there in the morning and gone at night. Irrational thoughts raced in my mind: *Maybe I can go to sleep and wake up from this nightmare. Perhaps Fofi will start moving in the hospital and they will realize she is still alive!* I fantasized about this last thought incessantly. I even had images of her getting up from her casket until the very moment we were at the burial and it disappeared into the ground.

Alain hugged me and silenced my most desperate thoughts. I don't remember what he said or where we slept. The details of that moment are a blur. It is amazing how the mind can protect us by hiding painful memories. I laid there in silence with my heavy eyes open. A part of me wanted to pause time so it would always be the last day I saw Fofi. The other part wanted to fast forward so I could die too and spare my soul from the pain. Minutes or hours later, my eyes and mind finally gave in and shut down.

The next thing I remember is being on the floor of my daughter's bathroom, rocking back and forth in the fetal position. I don't remember how I got there or what time it was. I vividly recall clawing at my hair in a desperate and futile attempt to get rid of my thoughts and flashbacks. They were unbearable. I kept replaying the nightmare by the pool. I was trying to make sense of what had occurred. I didn't understand.

How did Fofi end up at the bottom of the pool? Did she jump, fall, or try to swim to us and didn't make it? How could none of the many people there have seen her? What did she think during the seconds she was sinking down to the bottom of our pool? Was she wondering, "Where's Mommy? Why isn't she protecting me as she promised?" I remembered the moment by the steps at the Ritz Carlton's pool in Puerto RIco a week prior where I said, "Don't be scared, Fofi. Mami will take care of you."

But I didn't fulfill my promise. I didn't take care of my daughter when she let go of fear.

The thought of failing her produced a flood of emotions: guilt, pain, disbelief, terror, anger, frustration, confusion, and excruciating pain. These emotions haunted me all at once. For the first time in my life, I understood why people "go crazy." That was the moment of deepest despair and hopeless darkness I had experienced in my life. I couldn't fall asleep and staying awake was unbearable. I was trapped by monsters that tortured my brain. I thought I had hit rock bottom hours before, but rock bottom was even deeper now. I wanted my life to end so I wouldn't have to feel.

Suddenly my husband opened the bathroom door and it was as if an angel had come to rescue me. He kneeled on the floor beside me and held me in his arms. His embrace brought hope into the darkness, and I let myself cry. He lifted me up—literally—and took me back to bed. With his love and grace, Alain silenced my torment.

I learned years later that he also had racing thoughts at that moment, although different to mine. He wondered, *What can I do? I am not the one trained in psychology! If she's like this, what's going to happen to me?*

I was, indeed, the one who had clinical training. I took pride in leading by example and practicing what I preached. But not even a PhD in Clinical Psychology or the 13 years of experience I had at the time could prepare me for the loss of my sweetheart.

The devastating pain surpassed all knowledge. At that moment, I was not Dr. Betsy. I was just a human being; a mother enduring pain. Alain led me back to bed, where I finally fell asleep.

CHAPTER 4

Life After Death

The next morning, I woke up to a bright new day. The light of the sun shone in along the sides of the blackout shades and lit up the room enough to let me know that nothing had changed overnight. Fofi's bed was still empty.

How could the sun come up and people go about their day as if nothing had happened? I thought. I wanted life to stop for a minute so I could grieve. I was dead inside, so I couldn't stand seeing "life" around me. I felt the world was inconsiderate and unempathetic. *My daughter just died, World. Have a little compassion and stop everything. I need time to feel!*

Soon my anger turned to sadness. I remember thinking, *Today is the first day in almost three years that I will not see Fofi.* I smelled and hugged her safety blanket, hoping her scent would never go away. I didn't want to accept this new day because the one before was when she last smiled at me, kissed me, hugged me, made me laugh, and spoke to me with her adorable Hispanic accent. I felt like a teenager who was kissed on her cheek by her crush and didn't want to wash her face.

Saying goodbye to her last day of life felt like washing away that last kiss.

The details of that morning are a blur. I don't remember if I was the last one to wake or if Chichi and Alain were still sleeping. I don't know what time it was, nor do I recollect how I made it to the living room but I recall vividly what I saw then.

As soon as the hallway door flung open, there was a special man awaiting me the way I welcomed Fofi the morning prior. His arms were open, and his face revealed a shy, half smile. My eyes opened wide and my heart skipped a beat. I ran towards him. My arms were not long enough to wrap around him and squeeze him as hard as I wanted to.

It was my older brother.

He was the first face I saw from my family. Manolo is a tall, strong-willed man. I felt safe when he held me in his arms. His presence gave me comfort. I realized how important it was for me to have someone from my family of origin there.

I'm not sure if he said anything, but he didn't have to. His actions spoke loudly. Manolo learned about Fofi the night before, when my dad called him frantically. Still in shock, he felt the urge to leave immediately. He asked his wife to pack and get their 2-year-old and 4-month-old boys ready. "She's alone. Mom and Dad are in Puerto Rico. I have to be there. We are leaving right now," he told my sister-in-law. She followed his instructions without hesitation.

Within 15 minutes, he was on the road heading from Georgia to Miami to accompany me. He drove through the night and, 11 hours later, he arrived at my home. My brother-in-law let him in.

His loving gesture humbled me. You couldn't have paid me to drive that long with a newborn and yet, to him nothing mattered more than being there for me. Manolo's presence consoled me like no other.

My big brother brought me hope.

Something about his thoughtfulness moved me deeply at that moment of despair. I felt so loved.

Then I realized Chichi didn't have her sister to do the same for her. Ever.

She no longer had Fofi to bend time and space by traveling hundreds of miles in an instant to be there for her. She also wouldn't have a sister to welcome her with open arms the morning after a tragedy.

I had a flashback of Chichi's first day in Pre-K days prior. We went there as a family to drop her off. It was the first time Chichi would be away from her little sister for that many hours. They were each other's best friends and had been home together their entire lives.

Fofi sat on her big sister's lap at the table in her new classroom. Placing her hands on Fofi's face, Chichi pleaded, "Fofi, please give me lots of kisses because you have to leave."

"I don't want to leave. I want to stay with you," replied Fofi.

"But, Fofi, you can't stay here, so give me lots of kisses."

Looking back now, I feel like that farewell foreshadowed my daughter's fate.

Shortly after breakfast, Chichi asked, "Mami, when is Fofi coming home from the hospital?" I held back tears that wanted to pour out from my eyes. I just couldn't bring myself to tell Chichi about Fofi yet. To escape the situation, I said, "Chichi, let me get Papi," Together, we took her outside so we could be alone and away from our family members.

I can still see the sweet look on her face as she waited patiently for us to tell her when "her best friend" was coming home.

"My love, Fofi is not coming back. She is in heaven now," my husband said truthfully. Her eyes opened wide. Confused, she asked, "Not even in three days?" Despite my excruciating pain, I managed to answer, "No, my dear. Not even in three days." "Not even in seven days?" I shook my head no. "16 days? 23?" "No, Chichi, she's never coming home, but she will always be in your heart."

Her eyes dropped. Her glow faded. It was as if a shadow had covered her bright face and made it opaque. My heart sank, and I felt the unbearable pain that comes from witnessing a loved one grieve. I don't think she understood what this meant, but she knew enough to feel deeply saddened.

To distract her, Alain and I invited Chichi to go on a bike ride, one of her favorite things to do. On our way out of the neighborhood, a black pick-up truck on the main road turned onto our street and stopped abruptly. It surprised us to see José, our handyman, step out of his car and rush to give us a heartfelt hug. We were still processing what had just happened when he turned around and got back in his car. He didn't say a word. He didn't have to. His loving gesture showed that his heart was with us, and we felt it. José was a friend then, but at that moment he became family.

We rode bikes around the area, and it terrified me that what used to be a fun family activity was now a solemn experience. Chichi was mute and pensive.

All I could hear was the wailing despair in my heart.

As we made our way back to the house, I spotted dozens of cars in our driveway. I felt overwhelmed. I didn't have the strength to see anyone, so I went in through the garage. Alain escorted me to my room while trying not to seem rude. I've never despised being the center of attention more than at that moment (and many more to come). I was grateful for their support, but it was too hard to keep my composure.

I hid in my bedroom with Alain, while our guests entertained Chichi and Gordi with the toys and coloring books they brought. Our room felt too big and unsafe. I needed to be contained, so our walk-in closet became our shelter. The surrounding walls, covered by hanging clothes, protected us from being seen or overwhelmed by guests. The vanity on the left provided me with a sitting area, and the big mirror on that wall made the space feel ample and comfortable.

We let one visitor into our secret refuge that day: the priest who baptized all my children, and whom we love dearly. Although most of what I experienced during that time is a blur, I remember clearly the moments we spent sitting on the floor of my closet with Father Gerardo. Little did I know that his message would change my life forever. Alain and I sat, crossed-legged, begging for answers. *Why did this happen? How could God allow this?*

Father Gerardo didn't have the answers, but he assured me that God didn't do this *to us*. "He loves you too much to take her away and break your heart. Once she died, He did welcome her into His arms, but He didn't cause this to happen."

I was confused. *If God didn't do it, then why did she die?* Father Gerardo pulled a piece of paper from his pocket and drew two separate circles on it. In one he wrote, "Consequence" and in the other, "Mystery." Then he explained, "We can link some life events to our own doings, but others are a mystery. Getting lung cancer when you've been a smoker all your life may result from your smoking habit. But losing Fofi in a pool accident—despite giving her infant survival lessons, swimming classes, and constant supervision inside and outside the pool—is a mystery."

A part of me wanted to believe him, but I felt responsible. *How could this have happened? I was right there in the pool with her! So many people were around us!* I was the psycho-mom everyone criticized because I was so overprotective. I was in the pool because Fofi asked me to be there. I made sure she learned how to swim. I didn't get it. I was right there. Right there!

Father Gerardo insisted, "It's a mystery"—which essentially means we may never know how or why it happened. I believed him, but doing so raised another question: *If God didn't do this, then why didn't He prevent it?* This question remained in my mind for months.

Then, impatiently, Alain interrupted, "Father, you've seen this before. Will we ever be happy again?" Hope of experiencing joy again had vanished. Our solemn bike ride validated our fate.

Father Gerardo gently grabbed both of our hands. "Some people are happy again and others never find joy."

Agitated, Alain interrupted, "What's the difference?"

Father Gerardo replied, "The ones who are never happy again honor their children through tears and grief. They believe that the more they suffer, the more they love. Conversely, those who are happy again, understand that love is not measured by tears, and choose to honor their loved one through service, gratitude, and love." He gazed at us with mercy.

Father Gerardo's enlightened words suggested the choice was ours. I knew which type of parent I wanted to be. I would honor my daughter's life with joy and service. I didn't know how I was going to do it at the time, but I needed to believe I could.

In hindsight, that was the moment I chose joy.

CHAPTER 5

Celebration of Life

We were still sitting on the floor with Father Gerardo when some visitors interrupted. I looked up and saw my mom and dad with open arms. I got up in a heartbeat and rushed to their embrace. I cried on their shoulders like the little girl I once was. I felt safe for a moment.

After what seemed like minutes, I saw through my tears that my younger brother, Carlitos, and my sister-in-law stood right behind them. Carlitos stared at me without saying a word. He waited patiently to hug me next. As with my older brother, his presence soothed my aching heart. My family was complete.

My parents suggested that I eat something, but I had no appetite. They walked me over to the kitchen, hoping I'd be tempted by one of the treats people had brought. On my way there, I passed by lots of people who had come to support us. The details of who they were is a haze. I just know that many eyes followed me and I was scared to make eye contact.

Though humbled by their presence, I felt overwhelmed. In moments of crisis, I prefer being alone with my immediate family.

I don't want to feel the pressure of hosting or even talking. The thought of them seeing me so vulnerable was the equivalent of being stared at when walking around in the nude. I didn't feel safe in my own house.

I grabbed some water and rushed back to my bedroom to hide my naked pain. As I made way, my peripheral vision revealed that everyone gathered in groups talking among themselves, except *one person.*

There was a woman leaning against the 20-inch wall in my family room just below the A/C thermostat. She was alone. She wasn't on her phone. She was just *there.*

In the blur of that multitude, Caroline's presence stood out. I knew that her visit was *simply* motivated by her desire to be available to me. She wasn't there to find out more details about what happened. She didn't leave her husband and three little ones at home just to socialize. She didn't care to gage how bad I was doing. She was just *there*—standing quietly below the thermostat against the smallest wall in my home—waiting for me to need her.

Her quiet, yet strong presence caught my attention as I walked past her into the hallway. That image remained stuck in my mind and represented the beginning of a deepening friendship.

As I settled down in my bedroom, someone came to remind us we needed to start making funeral arrangements. She told us where to go and who to talk to.

My body left my bedroom and made its way across the hallway, towards the living room, and to the main entrance of our house. The people who were gathered in our home opened a path for us. I felt overwhelmed by the looks on their faces. Their "pity gaze" of sad eyes and low energy confirmed once again that this was really happening. It was devastating. I felt scared and unsafe. I clung to Alain and asked him to hold me tight. I felt cold even though it was a hot Miami summer day.

I finally made it to the car. Painful thoughts raced through my mind as my body slowly moved toward the funeral home office. *I can't believe I'm never going to see Fofi again. Do I really have to choose the box in which they'll bury her sweet body? As a grown woman, she was supposed to do this for me. Is this really happening? Wake up, wake up from this nightmare!*

Funeral Arrangements

I dreaded the traditional wake in which people show up to give their condolences and then sit around, reminiscing and laughing with friends they haven't seen since the last funeral. The thought of that scene infuriated me. I even imagined beating someone up if I heard laughter at Fofi's funeral. I felt a world of unpleasant emotions all at once. I was heartbroken, angry, numb, terrified, exhausted, and so weak that I could barely hold myself up.

After what seemed like the longest 15-minute car ride, we arrived at the funeral home. There, we sat down with the memorial counselor who was going to help us with the funeral arrangements. I would be lying if I said I remember exactly what happened in that meeting because I don't. I can barely remember what the room looked like. I do recall thinking *I don't know how this woman can have this job.* She was kind and compassionate, as much as one can be while talking about how to get rid of your beloved child's body.

Somehow, we came to an agreement. My husband must have done it all. The only thing I was clear about was *NO VIEWING*. I wanted to make sure that I didn't hurt anyone in my upset and I dreaded being vulnerable in front of hundreds of people. My closet seemed like a safer place to break down.

Another thing that kept me away from wanting a traditional viewing is the solemn feeling it has. Fofi was the happiest and funniest girl I knew. I didn't want to commemorate her death. I wanted to celebrate her life!

An hour later, we left the funeral home knowing how my daughter's casket would look. I was certain that I would find the strength to honor her life the way she deserved. I would offer the most beautiful Mass I could in her memory, and at the end we would allow people who adored her to speak about the immense joy she had brought them.

A friend set up a meeting for us with the pastor at St. Timothy Catholic Church, the parish we had recently joined after moving to our new neighborhood. Monsignor Marin welcomed us with great empathy and love. He gave us a heartfelt hug and escorted us to the office. The room of our encounter had a long conference table that took up most of the space. Alain and I were sitting across from the priest along the middle of the table, waiting for guidance. We felt lost.

He offered us his condolences and then expressed a great desire to help us in any way possible. His sincere kindness moved me, especially because this was the first time we had ever spoken to him. He treated us as if we were long-time parishioners.

I was so distraught; I couldn't bring myself to discuss the funeral Mass arrangements. Monsignor's warm-hearted disposition gave me permission to skip the logistics and share my thoughts. "Father, I keep trying to understand. I don't know how this could have possibly happened. I and so many others were right there in the pool! I keep getting torturous images of how Fofi got in the water. Did she jump? Did she fall? Did she slide into the deep end? Did she mean to swim to us to show off her swimming skills the way she had earlier that day?" Alain put his hand on my back, as I cried inconsolably.

Quavering, I continued, "I particularly obsess over the moment when she started sinking in the water. What did she feel? What did she think? I had told her a week before, 'Don't be afraid. Mami will take care of you'. Was she thinking about that? Did she feel I failed her? Did she suffer? Was she desperately gasping for air? How long did she struggle? Was she afraid? Did she feel abandoned and unprotected? I am drowning in these dark thoughts and still can't make sense of it. I can't find an answer to how this could have happened."

Msgr. Marín listened patiently to my rambling until I took a breath.

"Before I became a priest, I was a cardiologist."

Those words caught my undivided attention.

"Children don't suffer the way adults do when they drown. Just one quick gulp of water can fill their lungs and take their lives. Fofi didn't agonize the way you have been imagining."

The lump in my throat dissolved. The tightness in my chest softened. His words were exactly what I needed to hear.

Fofi didn't suffer the way I had been experiencing in the darkness of my thoughts. This wise priest understood that I needed a physician and a spiritual guide, not a funeral director.

I had longed for confirmation that she hadn't spent her last seconds of life dwelling on her mother's unfulfilled promise from the week prior: *Don't be afraid, Fofi. Mami will take care of you.*

The conversation gave me the peace and mental clarity to plan my daughter's Mass.

We wrapped up the details and left the meeting with the scriptures and complete agenda for the ceremony. It would take place in two days' time. It was Monday—the day after the accident—but I felt so overwhelmed and disoriented that the Mass on Wednesday seemed too far away. I needed that day to come so I could formally say farewell to my daughter and start figuring out what life would be without her.

Alain and I went home after the meeting. As if dealing with funeral arrangements wasn't hard enough, we had to host an uninvited visitor. The woman from the Department of Children and Families came back to our home. She interrogated us and our guests. She then gave herself permission to tour our home, as if looking for signs to prove we were responsible, loving parents. I understood this was part of the protocol, but it still hurt to think that anyone in the world could doubt my pure love and intentions toward my deceased child.

This may have been the hardest day of my life. Having to make important decisions when everything was a challenge and my suffering prevailed, seemed impossible. Choosing to donate your baby's organs, as well as her eyes and other body parts that would not be exposed in the closed casket, was agonizing. What was death to me, represented someone else's chance to live. This thought was confusing. It was both beautiful and painful.

I don't remember anything else from that day or the next. All I know is that family and friends came from everywhere. My house became increasingly crowded. I spent more time in the living areas on Tuesday, as my close relatives and loved ones arrived.

At some point, my phone rang. It was the counselor from my daughter's school. I cringed. *Was everything okay with Chichi?* She must have heard my thought because she started saying, "Everything is okay." She wanted me to know that a family from school offered to pay for Fofi's funeral. In case you don't fully understand what that means, some stranger was willing to give us over $10,000 out of the goodness of his/her heart. It's been many years since that phone call, and that family still remains anonymous. *If you are reading this now, please know that my heart will be forever grateful.*

On Tuesday night, Zuly and Vale came to my house to help me prepare a slideshow for Fofi's Celebration of Life. I had a hard time choosing pictures and videos, but they patiently guided me. Exhausted, and still in their work clothes at midnight, they acted as if there was no other place they would rather be.

Wednesday finally came. My parents, brothers, aunts, and cousins made those days bearable. Some joined us in a few more "walk-in closet conversations" like the one we had with Father Gerardo. These chats brought me hope.

Final Good-bye

That morning, the closet was my safe space to review the eulogy as my cousin fixed my hair. Nothing I had written seemed good enough to express my love for Fofi. I always thought I was good with words, but this time I was at a loss for them. I cried in disbelief as I prepared to say goodbye to my daughter publicly.

My family members helped get the kids ready for the Mass. We arrived at the church with only a few minutes to spare. Lots of people entered through the double doors. I caught a glimpse of a friend from Chicago. I couldn't believe she would travel for me. Her presence moved me. I also noticed a client whose gaze suggested I, her therapist, seemed more disoriented than she had ever been in a session. Other than them, I was too overwhelmed to recognize anyone.

I walked in holding on to Alain and avoiding eye contact to evade the terror of my reality reflected in people's faces. We worked our way through the crowd, to the front pew of the church. We sat in front of the delicate frame that held the picture of Fofi that I had chosen. This photo reflected her angelic countenance. The small white casket covered in white roses stood next to us, sheltering her resting body.

The Mass started and, even though I tried to be present and pay attention, I don't remember much. I do, however, recall Father

Gerardo's homily. He was brave enough to talk about water, the very element that took my daughter's life. He reminisced about the day he baptized her; how he poured holy water over her tiny 3-month-old head. He compared water to life because in the baptism it made her holy and, on her last day, it brought her to Heaven. His perspective brought peace to my dark feelings about "water." *Water didn't kill her. Water made her holy and gave her eternal life.* I caught myself repeating his hope-filled words in my mind.

Before the final blessing, it was time to share some words in Fofi's honor. Her grandparents, godparents, uncles, and friends went to the altar to speak. They all talked about how she made everyone's life better and gave specific examples to prove it.

Fofi was a character. She was sweet, noble, bubbly, and had a delightful sense of humor. She hadn't always been that way though. As a baby, Fofi was colicky and difficult. She was always crying and hard to comfort. This made it very difficult to find willing babysitters.

Over time, she became very attached to Chichi, her older and more easygoing sister. I never wanted her to feel left behind, so when someone volunteered to take care of Chichi, I would say, "They come in a package!" and sent both girls. Eventually, Fofi outgrew her colic and mommy-itis. Little by little, she also earned the love and admiration of our family and friends with her charismatic and sunny disposition.

On that day, though my pain was unbearable, a bit of joy dawned as I listened to others share stories about Fofi and how she stole their hearts. I relived memories that made me smile and was humbled by people's love for Fofi.

At last it was time for Alain and I to speak. We climbed up the stairs to the altar and turned around to face the pews. When I looked up, I saw hundreds of people filling up the church. People sat and stood, leaving no room for anyone else to enter. This was probably the time that I felt most humbled. These people had inconvenienced themselves on a Wednesday afternoon to be there for us.

In the split-second before I spoke, I thought about everything they must have had to put aside to share this moment with us: take time off from work, arrange for someone to pick up their kids at school, set up babysitting, and cancel prior commitments. Even though I can't fully grasp who was there, their presence touched me profoundly.

This validated an article I read in Reader's Digest titled *Never miss a funeral*. Though it may seem impractical to attend these events because the griever may never know you were there, your presence still matters. On behalf of myself and any other person you have been there for who remains oblivious to it, please accept our most heartfelt gratitude.

I don't remember whether I spoke first or if Alain did. I just remember that I was in awe as he spoke. He showed strength and vulnerability at the same time. His words and emotions portrayed the incredibly devoted and loving father that he is. Alain says I'm the poet of the family, but there is something powerful about his words. They may not be as extravagant or elaborate as I can make them seem, but they always come from the heart and exude wisdom. His message soothed my soul and reminded me how fortunate I was to have chosen such a good father for my Fofi. Because of Alain, her brief life was more full of love than that of others who live to see old age.

As soon as I started addressing the audience, a strong sense of calmness came over me. Contrary to the chaotic emotions I expected, I felt profound peace. My human self couldn't have spoken with such grace and strength about my beloved Fofi while in such pain. Although I felt tears running down my cheeks and my voice trembled, my spirit was mighty. I stood there—bold and confident—celebrating my daughter's life, not dwelling on her body's death.

Afterward, I heard many of our guests share that they too felt my peace and power; that it was my energy and Alain's that calmed *their* aching hearts. They said they went to support us, but left feeling it was we that soothed them. They couldn't comprehend—rationally—how we could stand tall in the joy that parenting Fofi brought, even though our lives had just been shattered by her loss. It was not *me* that held my body up and spoke with courage. I didn't have the strength to do so. What my guests said they experienced was the presence of divine power within me. To me, it was God. My heart is grateful for that moment. It gave me a great sense of satisfaction to feel that we had successfully celebrated our angel's life that day.

CHAPTER 6

Healing Begins

The Monday after Fofi's celebration of life, a family friend from our church came to our house with food. Ana was the first one to sign up for the food chain intended to show love and support to our family. With a humble heart, I engaged in conversation with her and asked, "How did this food chain come to be?" She explained that several ministries from our church came together to collaborate.

Ana belonged to the Ministry of Mothers Sharing, also known as MOMS, and Emmaus—a ministry for Christian women and men in Miami. My husband was also an Emmaus brother. To become an Emmaus brother or sister, one must complete their spiritual retreat.

"I have always wanted to attend, but was waiting for the right moment—a time when I was going through something difficult and needed spiritual strengthening..." I rolled my eyes as I said this, realizing I was at that moment. Ana said there was one coming up in less than a month, to which I replied, "Oh no, it's too soon. I'm not ready for that."

"You never know," she said softly, planting a seed in my mind.

Ana's *"You never know"* echoed inside me. Three weeks later, I was on my way to the retreat house feeling like a 4-year-old being dropped off on the first day of preschool—vulnerable, anxious and scared. On my way there, I cried helplessly in anticipation for the spiritual open-heart surgery that awaited me. Poor Alain. I can still see his helpless sad eyes when he left me and drove off that warm Friday in September.

By Saturday night, I felt the retreat surgery had been a success. Although I was still numb from the anesthesia of my denial, I fully experienced the presence of God within me. He relieved the unbearable flashbacks, hopelessness, guilt, and what if's that weekend.

I wish I could explain how I witnessed divine healing, but I would be minimizing His work if I tried. It was as if God lifted the brick that was crushing my heart. He shone His light within me. I left with a renewed spirit on Sunday, ready to focus on healing.

Healing, however, did not remove the pain. Just like a wound hurts after a malign tumor has been operated on, my heart ached right after the darkness was removed. The difference was that this time I knew the discomfort would go away because it was the pain of healing. Looking at the journey this way was mentally and physically more bearable.

HEALING BEGINS

When I didn't find the magical cure I was hoping for after the retreat, I sought tools that would provide relief. Words, hugs, smiles, and music became my medicine. A friend who went through a painful miscarriage gifted me a song that she thought would soothe me.

I will trust you, by Gary Chapman, was a song about a grieving father who could only feel pain and longed for his own death after losing his daughter. I sure was able to relate. What made this song meaningful to me was the hope it conveyed. Amidst his deep pain, Chapman acknowledged God's presence in his life and trusted Him, just as I chose to.

I can't sing. I don't even sing in the shower, but when I heard this song, my lips involuntarily moved with beautiful intonation. This song was written for me. I was enduring extreme pain and fervent faith at the same time. As crazy as I thought God was for allowing my Fofi to die, I knew His plans for me and for her were better than my own. I trusted Him. I just asked that He help me make sense of things with my limited human mind.

I needed to understand why God allowed this to happen. I knew He hadn't done this to Fofi, or me, because I was clear that a God of love and mercy didn't have it in Him to induce pain. What I often wondered, however, was why He hadn't intervened to save her. I faithfully begged Him for an answer. He sent the message through my Mother.

I was visiting my mom in Daytona when we gathered around the kitchen to chat. She is a very wise woman of faith. She always seems to have the right answer for every spiritual question I ask, so I put her to test once more. "Mami, I cannot understand why God saved other kids in near-drowning situations, and not my Fofi. I was raising her for Him and I was a responsible mom. I deserved a chance." Mom responded with a story.

"I know another woman who also lost her daughter tragically," she said. "Her suffering grew stronger as did her resentment toward God. One day she had a powerful vision of her daughter's life if she had survived. She saw her daughter as a prostitute, lost, and suffering excruciating emotional pain. at that moment, she realized God did save her from a lifetime of suffering." My mom paused and then continued, "Betsy, God is a better dad than you are a mom, if you can imagine that. He wants the absolute best for His children and, ultimately, the best thing is that they are able to enjoy eternal life. If intervening to save Fofi would have helped her become more ready for Heaven, he would have saved her; but if she was ready and staying would have exposed her to suffering, then He had no business intervening."

This explanation made sense to the part of me that insisted on understanding the mysteries and making the infinite finite. It may be the greatest lesson my mother ever taught me because, to this day, it still resonates. In every unpleasant experience I have, I find myself reciting, If God does not intervene, there is a purpose, because His plans for me are better than mine.

CHAPTER 7

The Birth of A Rainbow

Before Fofi's accident, Alain and I had planned a couples' trip to St. Augustine, Florida. It was scheduled for October, so we debated whether to cancel, but finally opted to go. That city is very meaningful to us because it is home to the first shrine dedicated to Our Blessed Mother in the United States: Our Lady of La Leche. In it, there's an image of Mary nursing infant Jesus. People go there to ask Mother Mary to intercede with Jesus to grant them healthy pregnancies and deliveries.

Alain and I went for the first time before we had children. We prayed that Jesus would bless my womb and make me fertile. Months later, two lines showed up on my pregnancy test. Then, we went again when I was pregnant with Chichi, later with Fofi, and then Gordi. Fofi was with us during our previous visit.

The night before we left for St. Augustine, Alain and I had a huge upset. We were in our room packing while talking about how unnerving Fofi's accident had been. *Why didn't we see what happened? We were right there!* At some point I mentioned all the other people that were around who didn't notice her being in danger either. Alain snapped angrily, "Don't try to blame others. It will always be our fault. *We* were responsible for taking care of Fofi and we couldn't even keep her alive."

This unexpected blow left me gasping for air. *How could he say that to me?* I had worked hard to overcome the guilt I felt about her death. *I'm not going there again,* I thought. I stared at him in disbelief. I stood there, paralyzed, hoping he would take it back. He didn't. He turned around and stormed out of our room.

My knees buckled and I sobbed. I grabbed a red pillow that my friend gave me at the Emmaus retreat for moments of despair. I knelt on it. *Please help me, God. Give Alain a sign—a sign so big and undeniable that it will help him get rid of any self-blaming thoughts and reunite us emotionally.*

I realized that Alain didn't say those words to hurt me, nor was he playing the victim card. He is the most accountable man I have ever met. This was his way of assuming responsibility for our daughter and preventing me from blaming others for her loss—a temptation I must have suggested during our argument, which I vulnerably confess to as I write this.

I wasn't as good as he was at accountability back then. I did engage in the blame game secretly, as I desperately searched for understanding. Alain is a very rational man. Accepting responsibility himself was an act of accountability for him, not a way of victimizing himself. In his mind, this was a truth he arrived at by reason. *God had entrusted Fofi to us and we had failed to protect her from danger that day. Period.*

Being more of an emotional thinker, I struggled with that perspective. Lacking insight about how we processed differently, I felt he hadn't caught up to me in the healing of guilt, and I kept thinking in prayer *He has to meet me where I am because I'm not going back there.* The thought of not being on the same page with him filled me with dread.

Alain was my partner, my confidant, my strength. Our togetherness is what brought consolation to our daily grief. "No one understands me, but you," he would often say in our weeping sessions. In a weird way, that statement brought me peace. I was able to bring him hope because he felt accompanied and validated. We were each other's shoulder to cry on. This disagreement threatened desolation, which terrified me. Alain and I were a team. Whenever we weren't on the same page, I felt lost and weak. That night, those feelings were more staggering than ever before.

Alain and I decided to leave our argument unresolved that night. We slept on it and woke up with a better attitude. Despair was also less dramatic on my end. We were determined to have a good trip, so we decided to postpone resolving this disagreement.

That Friday morning, our friends met us at our house, and off we went to St. Augustine. Four hours later, we stopped at my parents' house in Daytona for a much needed hug and a delicious home-cooked meal. It was so nice to see them. It was hard to have them far away in times like these. Finally, we arrived at The Saragossa Inn, our favorite Bed and Breakfast in St. Augustine, with time to enjoy that gorgeous town.

After dinner and some live music, I found myself unable to resist my urge to sleep. I figured I was still drained from the night before and the trip. The boys weren't ready to call it a night, so I literally laid down on two chairs and fell asleep in a bar. When I woke up, my girlfriends went with me to the hotel and our husbands met us shortly after.

The next morning, as I got ready for the day, I came across an old leftover pregnancy test in my toiletry bag. As I stared at it, an inner voice told me to do the test and look at it with Alain when we got to the Shrine of Our Lady of La Leche. *Oh please!* I thought, *How ridiculous*. I had no reason to believe I was pregnant.

As you can imagine, during those times of grief, sexy times were few and far in between. Alain and I were mindful of nurturing our relationship, but we often found ourselves crying together despite our hope for another kind of togetherness. The point is that the possibility of being pregnant again seemed truly unreasonable, but I went with it anyway.

I often struggled with discerning what came from my desires and what came from God, but I always erred on the side of safety.

If this was God speaking to me, I was going to listen. If it was my own mind, then the worst that could happen was that I made a fool of myself, and I was okay with that too. I took the pregnancy test and, without looking at it, placed it in my jeans' back pocket.

After an amazing breakfast at the B&B, we finally arrived at the much-anticipated shrine. It is surrounded by vibrant greenery, lush trees, and gorgeous flowers. When we walked towards it, we were welcomed by the clean scent of nature and the soothing caress of the wind. The salty smell from the beautiful blue waters of the Intercoastal greeted us warmly. I felt a strong sense of peace and noticed a smile involuntarily form on my lips. I was happy to be there.

Alain and I walked into the quiet shrine and knelt down to pray. When my eyes closed, my vision sharpened. I could see Fofi clearly in that place. She had been there with us just a year before. She had caressed her brother in my womb and prayed with us for his wellbeing. Reliving that memory created great pain in my heart and I sobbed irrepressibly.

Alain extended his arm to pull me closer to him. Later, I learned that his experience at that moment was quite different. Rather than reminiscing about the last time we were there *with Fofi*, he prayed and asked God to bless my womb and allow it to be fertile one more time.

You see, Alain and I thought we were all done having babies. I had been either pregnant or breastfeeding nonstop for five and a half years. Although we are both one of four siblings and originally thought we wanted four children ourselves, we were ready for a well-deserved break. Alain and I had made the non-Catholic, rational decision that we would get a vasectomy. We had scheduled it for the week after Fofi's accident. Our possibilities of having a fourth child solely resulted from cancelling that doctor's appointment after Fofi passed. We didn't know what we wanted anymore, and it wasn't the right time to make important life decisions.

After some heartfelt weeping and praying, we exited the chapel and felt replenished by the soothing wind that softly caressed our faces. Our friends waited in a gazebo nearby with a shy smile that non-verbally communicated, "We are here for you." I smiled back and sat next to them on a bench under that roofless structure adorned with vines. My friends looked at each other and smiled. We all felt the same calming peace.

I asked my friends if they would accompany me to pray a rosary for Fofi. In Puerto Rico there is a Catholic tradition of praying the rosary for nine successive days—known as the *novena*—as an offering for the eternal rest of a loved one who passed. In Miami, however, this is not a tradition, so I never got around to it. It was too hard anyway. This day, in that nature-filled setting, I was inspired to pray a rosary in memory of my daughter.

As our friends accompanied us in prayer, a profound sense of peace overwhelmed us. The natural air stroked our faces gently, and the foliage danced to the melody of the wind, producing background music. It was so beautiful! My heart felt soothed when we finished the rosary.

Suddenly, I remembered the pregnancy test I was carrying in my back pocket! I asked Alain to walk back to the shrine with me. I felt embarrassed to present him with that white stick and make such a show for nothing. I was overcome with doubt as we walked over, but my body continued to move. We entered the chapel and stood by the red candles they had for people to light in prayer offerings.

I built my courage and proceeded, "Baby, I have no reason to believe this is even possible, but this morning I felt compelled to do a pregnancy test and look at it here with you." Alain looked at me with a face that said, "You're crazy," a thought he often has about me. I continued anyway. "I know this sounds ridiculous, and I'm probably making a fool of myself, but I had to do it." I reached back to my right pocket and grabbed the long, thin, white stick. I handed the test to him and waited for his reaction, expecting disappointment.

It only took a second for him to examine the pregnancy test dubiously, but it felt like forever. I fixed my eyes on his facial expression. He seemed confused. "Two lines means positive?" he asked incredulously. His eyes continued to stare at it. *What is he saying? Could it be possible? Is he playing around?* I pulled the test out of his hands and looked at it with my own eyes. Holy Mother of God! I was pregnant!

My eyes and jaw opened wide in disbelief. I must've jumped up and down a few times before reaching for a hug. We couldn't believe it. The joy that rushed through my body overshadowed the pain I had experienced minutes earlier. I was ecstatic. This was, without a doubt, the greatest miracle I had ever witnessed. My heart was full and my smile was radiant.

Tons of thoughts rushed through my mind. *Is this the answer to my prayer about giving Alain a sign? Did Fofi have something to do with this?* At that moment, I didn't know that Alain had been praying for God to bless my womb with another baby. I knew from a conversation we had while crying together in bed, that having another child was the only thing that could help him understand why Fofi had to go. It was what could help his human mind make sense of our loss. After all, it was her death that changed our minds about following through with the vasectomy.

I was in awe and excited, but I had no doubt that this was really happening because I believe in miracles. Alain, however, couldn't believe it—*literally*. He kept asking, "But are you sure that's right? Do you have another pregnancy test?" *There goes my skeptical better half again,* I thought.

I had never been so eager to prove something to Alain. My girlfriends and I left the guys at a cigar lounge in downtown St. Augustine and drove to find the closest CVS. When we got there, I rushed to the Feminine Care section and there it was, the pregnancy test that would leave no room for doubt. It was one that read *pregnant* or *not pregnant*, instead of playing the single-double line guessing game. I knew I was pregnant for sure. That explained why I was so tired the night before when I passed out at the bar.

My heart was pounding as I silently asked *Fofi, give me a sign if you had something to do with this*. Looking back, my need to know that Fofi advocated for this pregnancy doesn't make much sense. However, at the moment, I felt I needed permission to feel the immense joy I was experiencing.

I paid for the test and walked out the double doors. It was a beautiful sunny day, but I felt tiny drops of rain coming down as we headed back to the car. I was continuing to ask for a sign when, suddenly, a rainbow appeared in the sky. I stood in the middle of the parking lot staring up at the colorful arch. I was in awe of what I felt was the sign from my Fofi. An electric current of bliss rushed through my entire body. In that instant, I couldn't even feel the pain for which I had shed tears just a couple of hours before. It had been replaced by the hope of new life in my womb and the sign of love that shone from the sky.

Without saying a word, my friends followed my stare and knew in an instant what was happening. They told me to snap a picture so I could always have that moment with me. And I did.

My friends and I went back to the bed-and-breakfast, so I could use the bathroom to take my second pregnancy test. This time, I waited impatiently to see the results with my friends. The word "pregnant" showed up on the tiny screen.

I looked up at the girls and gasped, "Oh my gosh, this is really happening!" The three of us literally jumped up and down. We couldn't wait to share the news with our husbands, so we went back to the cigar lounge to find them. I rushed to show Alain, who was waiting for me with a smile, and said, "Baby, it's confirmed!" After staring joyfully at the word *pregnant* for a second, he hugged me with great tenderness. As our bodies embraced, our hearts touched and synced. We didn't have to say a word to know what we were feeling. We were filled with gratitude. At that moment, we felt like the luckiest people on Earth.

CHAPTER 8

The Day-to-Day

The weeks following our trip to St. Augustine were a roller coaster. One moment I was ecstatic about the pregnancy; the next I felt guilty about my joy, so I reverted to sadness. I wanted to celebrate life, but I wasn't ready to stop grieving death.

It was like the very moment I clutched Fofi against my chest to rescue her from the bottom of the pool. As I tried to move up to the surface, the water resistance pushed me down. This time, the water was my grief. The idea that one must not feel moments of joy while mourning a loved one held me back. This lie consumed me and prevented me from keeping my head above water. It triggered thoughts that threatened to bring back the darkness of guilt and doubt. *Will Fofi feel that I'm replacing her with the baby? Is it wrong to feel happy about this new life? Is it too soon? Can I do this?* It was exhausting.

I needed help to stay afloat and I received it from my family, starting with my husband.

Alain was my lifesaver. I've always loved this man with my entire being. I admire and respect him more than any other human in my life. He inspires me to be better because better is what he deserves as a wife. Since the day we met, I've been devoted to making him the happiest man on earth, even when "happy" didn't seem to be in the cards for us.

Alain and I grieved and healed the loss of our daughter differently. I sat with my pain and shared it openly with anyone who would listen. He cried in private and didn't bring up the subject. I looked at Fofi's pictures and videos every chance I got. Though painful, it soothed me. Alain refrained from doing so because it hurt too much.

I believe in signs, angels, and even make-believe stories that can help me heal. My husband, on the other hand, is more skeptical and practical, which made my efforts to assist his healing unsuccessful. In spite of this, we took the time to share our process almost daily and honored each other's way of coping. I never expected him to grieve like me and he accepted my ways without judgment.

Every night, we sat on our bed and talked about our day. I told him about my thoughts, feelings, and triggers. He listened. Then I asked about him. He wasn't as descriptive. At first, our conversations resembled the unproductive small talk I have with my kids when I pick them up from school these days. I ask, "How was your day," and they just reply, "Fine." It was like pulling teeth. Then, I got creative with questions like, *"What was your favorite part of today?," "In what moments did you think about*

Fofi?," "How did you react?," "Do you have any "Ed" Stories?"

Ed was Alain's work colleague and friend. He is the kind of guy that will make you laugh without even trying. Sharing anecdotes about Ed made it easy for Alain to reveal his grief without feeling vulnerable and exposed. "I was crying in my office, as I do every morning, when Ed interrupted. Suddenly, I went from painfully crying one moment to being in tears of laughter the next."

I smiled every time I heard an "Ed story." He helped heal Alain's grieving heart through humor. All I had to do was listen and laugh with him.

I also remembered to love him every day. As a couples' therapist, I was aware of the disheartening statistics of marriages that fail after the loss of a child. Alain was my partner, my rock. I didn't want to live without him. I was mindful of being affectionate and intimate with him, even when all I wanted was to curl up into a ball and cry.

A week after Fofi's death, we went on a dinner date for our 7th wedding anniversary. It was the saddest, most solemn date I have ever been on, but we celebrated it nonetheless. We cried and grieved together. That moment was more intimate than our bodies touching. However, we engaged in the latter too.

Intimacy those days wasn't as passion-driven or frequent as it was when our hearts rejoiced. Instead, it was a beautiful way of connecting with Alain and reminding each other through physical contact that we were in this together—*literally*. Intimacy was a way of feeling safe as we held each other in a deep embrace.

Our efforts created a synergy in our relationship that allowed us to stay present with our kids. From the very beginning, I was determined to care for and celebrate my Chichi and Gordi. I had heard stories of bereaved siblings who felt emotionally abandoned by their grieving parents. "I wish I was the one who died so my mom would care about me," I heard a 13-year-old girl say months after her sister died of cancer. That was not going to be my story. I wanted my kids to feel my love, above my pain.

When Fofi passed, my son Gordi was almost one. His dependence on me literally forced me out of bed. I was still responsible for his nourishment and safety. We called him *Wreck-It Ralph*, because he was extremely active and also broke things like Ralph from the children's movie by the same name. Gordi started walking at nine months and was quite a handful!

There were times I would see him climb the couch and felt paralyzed instead of jumping out of my feet to keep him from falling. I'm embarrassed to confess I had irrational thoughts that didn't make me a good caretaker: *What's the worst that can happen? He's not going to DIE.* I was out of it, but I was there. Gordi kept me busy in more ways than one. I watched over him while he tore up the playroom, but I also contemplated him, when he slept like an angel. I loved that his chest moved with each breath, unlike Fofi's that night at the hospital.

Gordi looked a lot like his sister. He had tanned skin and dark brown eyes and hair. As he grew older, the resemblance was more than physical. When he started talking, he spoke exactly like her. He substituted c for t and had a high-pitched tone of voice, as did Fofi.

The days when her absence felt unbearable, I closed my eyes and I listened to Gordi. Although I knew—and loved—that it was him speaking, his voice soothed me like a song of angels. It was as though God had left a piece of Fofi in her brother.

Gordi also has his sister's kind-hearted spirit. He naturally gives love and compassion to people who feel invisible. Like Fofi, he has the gift of making others feel special. He helps me imagine what she would've been like at his age.

Chichi was the one I worried about most. She and Fofi had a deep connection, and I wanted to safeguard her spirit. Chichi used to share a bedroom with her sister. I loved watching their interactions through the video camera and still have images replaying in my mind.

When Fofi woke up, she sat up in her bed and peeked over the bed rail at Chichi. If her sister was still sleeping, she would lay down again to wait for her; but if Chichi wasn't there, she'd bounce out of bed like a rocket. Alain often said, "It's like they are one." It still feels that way.

Death didn't break their bond. When we told Chichi that her sister lived in her heart, she believed us. She continued to talk about her as if she was never gone. Her actions revealed she truly believed Fofi lived on.

My love for Chichi inspired me to do things that I would otherwise not feel ready for. Within a month of the accident, I redecorated her bedroom with a princess theme while she was in school.

I hired a team to help me paint, put a mural wallpaper with all Disney princesses, and add touches of royalty everywhere. On the walls to each side of her bed, there was a mirror frame with pictures of Chichi and Fofi dressed as princesses. We removed Fofi's bed and my mom helped me put away her clothing. I saved it.

The excitement of imagining Chichi's face when she saw her majestic room overpowered the pain of vanishing the physical belongings that still had Fofi's DNA.

When Chichi arrived home from school, we told her we had found a note from Fofi. I read it to her, "Dear Chichi, I wanted to tell you that I have a beautiful Princess room in heaven and I would love to give you our entire room so you can have your own. I decorated it with other angels because a princess like you deserves a beautiful castle. I love you so much, Chichi. I miss you. Your little sister, Fofi."

Chichi smiled and ran to her room. The look in her face…She was in awe.

She touched each princess in the wall and grabbed a doll of Jasmine laying on her pillow. She hugged it, looked at the ceiling, and whispered, "Thank you, Fofi."

I envied the innocence with which she believed it was her sister that gifted her the princess room. I wished I was four.

Days later Chichi got sick. I checked her temperature at 5 am and her fever had spiked. The next allowed dose of medicine was two hours away, so I went back to my room and prayed desperately.

Fever and I don't get along. My oldest sister was born healthy but developed complications that led to severe mental retardation and epilepsy. It all started with a high fever that evolved into a coma and brain damage, so you can imagine the fear that symptom brings to me. Besides, the dread of losing another child was a constant thought those days.

I struggled with the decision between giving her medicine before it was due or risking fever-induced complications. As I begged God to guide me, Chichi screamed loudly, "Mami, mami!" I sprang out of bed, ran to the end of the hall and into her room. She was sitting up on her bed.

Trying to sound calm, I asked, "What happened, my love?"

Excited, she shouted, "Mami, Mami, I can feel Fofi in my heart!"

My heart stopped.

"Chichi, what do you mean?" I asked.

She grabbed my hand, put it on her chest and said, "Mami, can you feel her?"

Her heart was racing.

"Yes, my dear, I can feel Fofi too."

I smiled at the uncanny confirmation that Chichi was being protected from above. More at ease, I went back to bed to wait until I could give her the next dose of medicine. Two hours later, the Advil never came out of the cabinet because her fever was gone.

CHAPTER 9

Thanks-giving

Chichi and Fofi continued to be connected way past their physical separation. Something special happened on Halloween, which reminded me of this truth.

Chichi didn't have her "twinsie" to match. They loved wearing the same outfits and had been the cutest Hello Kitties the year prior. Chichi agreed to be Rapunzel, which was one of the princess dresses she already had at home. *Thank God*, I thought to myself, because I didn't feel like shopping for just *one* girl costume. What struck me most about this special date wasn't the memories and costume ordeal. It was how Chichi handled it. I wasn't the only one missing Fofi, and I sure didn't cope with it as gracefully as my daughter did.

When Chichi arrived from school, she asked to go to the backyard. I thought she wanted to play, so I went out with her while her brother woke up from his nap to play too. I followed her as she walked past the play area. *Where was she going?* I noticed she wasn't engaging with me, so I gave her some space and went to pick up some balls and toys in the basketball court—by the avocado tree. She went to the other side of that big lush plant, which we baptized as "La Fofi Tree" because she used to climb it and jump from it into her daddy's arms.

La Fofi tree had a wind chime that someone gifted me after her passing. It read: "In loving memory of Verónica Isabel Guerra," her real name. Every time I listened to the angelic chime sound in the wind, I heard in my mind a, "Hi Mami," that made me smile. I always replied, "Hi, my sweet Fofi. God bless you, my love." The tree also had a butterfly sign. Next to it was a chair, where I would sit to pray and connect with my daughter daily.

I observed Chichi as she sat in the chair and spoke, looking up at the tree. *Who was she talking to?* I walked closer pretending to pick up a ball that I dropped close to her intentionally. Discreetly, I heard her say, "How is Heaven? Do you also have Halloween up there? What are you dressing up as? I'm gonna be Rapunzel, but the one that gets married with the white dress. You can wear the purple one if you'd like. I have a picture of you with that one in my room and you look like the most beautiful princess. I miss you, Fofi. I love you. Happy Halloween!"

My heart softened. I dried up my tears and approached her. She was peaceful and happy. She smiled and said, "Mami, I was asking Fofi what she's wearing for Halloween." I smiled back and thought, *Wow, we really ought to be like children.* She reminded me of *The Little Prince,* a classic novel I read in school about life from the perspective of a child. One of the most beautiful lessons in that book was told by a fox to the little prince, "It is only with the heart that one can see rightly; what is essential is invisible to the eye." Chichi saw and spoke to Fofi with her heart. *If only I could see rightly like her.*

This set up the tone for a more pleasant Halloween. We went out as a family to trick or treat around the neighborhood. Being Gordi's first year collecting candy on his own two feet made it an adventure. My little *Wreck-It Ralph* was roaming free and stuffing his face with candies. I still smile when I think about how ecstatic he was, oblivious to the pain his parents were enduring. Gordi's joy was contagious, and we did nothing to avoid feeling it too.

Thanksgiving

Thanksgiving came three months after Fofi passed. It's my favorite holiday and the one time a year I know for sure I'll be with my entire family. My siblings and parents are spread apart in different states, so knowing that I will be with them is one of the greatest gifts I look forward to every year. We always come up with excuses to be together, but Thanksgiving is our signature and non-negotiable excuse.

Every year, we meet at my older brother's house in Georgia and have what we call an "American Thanksgiving," our absolute favorite! We decorate the table with orange Fall leaves and pine cones from the backyard, cook two whole turkeys, make a yam side dish, and bake delicious pumpkin and pecan pies. We eat outside in the chilly weather, which we don't have in Miami or Puerto Rico, and then gather around a bonfire to tell stories. The cousins play outdoors. The warm-blooded Miamians are all bundled up, while my Georgian nephews wear shorts and short sleeves. The next day we go to a farm to cut the Christmas tree and are served warm apple cider and hot chocolate. The old antique cars in the entrance and the diverse pine trees are the perfect background for our Christmas Card pictures. It's the perfect holiday, or at least it was, until this one.

My incomplete family and I flew to Atlanta to spend Thanksgiving with my parents, siblings, and nephews. It was my first time seeing them after the funeral. I struggled deeply. A part of me felt discomfort with the way they looked at me, trying to gage how I was doing and whether or not I was about to fall apart. This may have been in my mind because they really did a phenomenal job in treating me as "normal" as possible.

I also had a hard time seeing my nephews play with my surviving children. The picture seemed incomplete. Fofi was very close and affectionate with them. She adored playing with her cousins! I hated not having her there. I was constantly reminded of her absence.

I couldn't connect with anyone. I felt I didn't belong. I was lonely, even though I was surrounded by *the* people I longed to be with the most. I was sad, so sad. Even as I write this, I struggle with keeping the tears from escaping my eyes. I can almost taste the pain and agonizing void of those days.

While I revisit that moment to access details so I can share them with you, I see myself in the basement bedroom of my brother's old house. That was the equivalent of my walk-in closet at home. I spent a lot of time there. I laid alone on a queen-sized bed, where I cried, slept, lamented, and thought about how I couldn't find anything to feel grateful for this *Thanks-giving*. The dark, windowless room was perfectly aligned with the way I felt inside.

The time came to share our Thanksgiving Lunch and pray as a family. I'm good with words, so I am usually the designated one to lead us in prayer or come up with a cute activity to encourage all others to share. This time I was at a loss. I forced myself to find something I was grateful for. I'm not sure if I succeeded. All I recall is that Alain and I cried a lot during our prayer, and many shared the same sentiment.

Later that day, my family gathered to pray in the living room. We often do this thing where we grab a scripture from the Bible and share our interpretation and how it relates to our lives. Being the open book that I am, and despise having pink elephants in the room, I shared my raw pain vulnerably. I must've shown some of the darkness that I was enduring those days because my dad felt compelled to "console" me in his rigid "Christian" ways.

I mentioned earlier that my dad is not one to express his feelings. He is rational and level-headed. He has a hard time empathizing when one feels something different to what he thinks a devoted Christian should experience. That's why it was so powerful for me that he reacted in a human way when I called him and gave him the news about Fofi's passing. I'll never forget that moment. At that instant, I had the emotionally available dad I always longed for. He was human and real; not just a Christian doing and feeling what he's "supposed" to.

This time, during our prayer gathering, my dad proceeded as usual. He gave me his sermon about what I was supposed to think and feel with the "blessing" of having a daughter in Heaven. I know he meant well, but at the moment I interpreted it as invalidating and unempathetic. My dad didn't understand the process that grief and faith entailed for me. I needed to feel the pain before I was ready to appreciate the silver lining of my loss.

Fortunately for me, I didn't have to defend myself because my older brother came to my rescue. He was infuriated by my dad's approach and stopped him. "She is entitled to feel that way. I am angry myself at how God could allow this," he said furiously and stormed out.

[Crickets].

Our prayer session ended. Although I felt bad for the outcome of what was supposed to be a unifying family activity, I was humbled by my brother's empathy.

What People Say

I am grateful for what this and other similar experiences taught me. Our family and friends say things that hurt or bother us when we are in pain. They seem unempathetic and dismissive. The truth is, however, that they are usually trying to be helpful. They want to see us happy now, so they fail to validate and honor the part of the process we are in.

It is hard to see a loved one suffer. People, then, try to remove the pain that we *must* endure to heal. They operate out of fear and are uncomfortable seeing us grieve. They say the unthinkable to change our perspective and try to shake the pain off.

"God needed an angel in Heaven", people would say trying to console me. *Really? Doesn't He have enough angels already?* Other times I heard, "She's in a better place." *Better than the heaven we had at home? Does that mean I should wish death upon my other children so they are "better" too?*

"Good thing you have other kids," was a common one, as if anyone could fill the void my Fofi left. Humans are not replaceable. Ever.

With the same desire to fast forward past our pain, family and friends judged us by their own standards or how they think they would respond if they were in our shoes. "It's been six months; you should be feeling better by now... It's time to give away all of her stuff... If I were you, I would have acted differently... It's not good for you to be watching her videos and pictures." *Says who?!*

They want to determine when enough is enough, but that's not up to them. Each grieving process is unique. I responded with grace to most undesirable comments, but I hurt inside.

I felt judged when my friend told her husband, "That's why I never keep my eyes off of my daughter." *Liar! That's impossible. Try having more than one kid. I want to see how you manage looking at different places at a time.* A week later, I learned her girl climbed on top of a glass piece of furniture while she was *not* looking, which could have ended in a tragedy.

People witness a misfortune like mine and their instinct is to explain the mystery. Unconsciously, they need to know exactly what went wrong to ensure that it won't happen to them. This comes from a place of fear, and the false belief that we can control everything. We can't.

Another common phrase I heard often was, "You are so strong." This outraged me. They meant it as a compliment, but what I heard was, "I admire you because you lost your daughter."

THANKS-GIVING

In my mind, that was the reason I demonstrated this "strength" they were talking about.

I felt like telling them, "You can shove your compliment up your behind. I would rather have my daughter back than your admiration. And, besides, how do you know I'm not falling apart behind closed doors? I'm not strong."

I guess people couldn't win with me those days. I understood later on what they meant. Though I didn't have it all together, I never gave up on life. They also saw in me the grace of the Holy Spirit when He helped me respond with the peace that "surpasses all understanding" (Philippians 4:7). Maybe I *was* strong after all.

There were times in which people didn't say anything. They were so uncomfortable with pain that they ignored it. Or maybe they didn't want to fall into the category of those who said the "wrong" thing. These friends spoke to me about irrelevant matters, but never addressed my grief. Their avoidance sounded like, "I don't care enough about you to acknowledge your pain."

Others simply disappeared. I have a friend who was there the day of the accident, but never showed up afterward. I was standing by the pool begging God to save my little girl when my gaze met her panic-stricken eyes. She stood on the other side of the backyard as a spectator. She clutched her son against her chest, terrified. For months I had flashbacks of that image. I waited and hoped that she would text, call, or visit me, but she never did.

Years later, she came to me for professional help with her marriage. During our sessions, I found out that my tragedy affected her so deeply that she didn't have the courage to reach out to me. She didn't know what to say or do.

What she didn't realize is that her inaction hurt me more than any wrong thing she could have ever said or done.

We tell ourselves we don't reach out when someone is going through divorce, loss, disease, or any other misfortune because we don't want to distress them. The truth is that we are not there for them because *we* are uncomfortable with their vulnerability. We avoid them because *we* don't have the solution to their problems, and it hurts *us* to see them grieving. We avoid them because we don't want to feel *their* pain.

Showing up when we have the power to fix the hardship feeds our ego but being there when all we have to give is our presence, humbles us.

My loved ones had a desperate urge to say something that would miraculously make me feel better, but nothing they said would bring my Fofi back. That's all I wanted early on.

They were at a loss because I had set them up for failure. I didn't need words or actions. All I wanted was for them to be *there,* simply holding space.

That's why the image of Caroline, the woman standing alone under the thermostat, captivated me. She was *there* the day after the accident and was present way past the shock of my daughter's passing.

Caroline reached out regularly to make sure I knew she was still *there*. She listened, cried, and let me cry. At times, she seemed uncomfortable reaching out. This was evidenced by comments such as, "I was scared to call you because I didn't know what to say...I hesitated to text you...I was afraid my message would remind you of the pain...I don't know what to do, but I feel compelled to be with you today."

Caroline cared enough to sit in the dark with me. She taught me that all we have to do to show love during adversity is to *be there*. We don't need to have the right words or fix anything. We get to be okay with the high possibility of screwing up by saying the wrong thing at the worst timing.

Being there is about accompanying the griever with empathy. Caroline's presence indicated that I could count on her. She had never lost a loved one, but her compassion and solidarity was healing. As Carl Rogers described, "When...someone really hears you without passing judgement on you, without trying to take responsibility for you, without trying to mold you, it feels damn good!"

People constantly ask me how they can support someone who lost a child. I realize they don't understand what empathy truly means. Empathy is the ability to share the feelings of another. We connect with the emotion, not the situation that exacerbated it.

The key people who demonstrated great empathy to me, had never lost a child. However, they understood pain. They were able to put themselves in my shoes and connect with my ache. That's what *being there* is all about.

I had people, including strangers and acquaintances from my community of faith, who hugged me randomly. Many told me that they were praying for me. I prayed every night, but I was too busy asking God for my loved ones to remember what others were going through. Hearing that they thought about me, in such an intimate moment, humbled me. I now pray for strangers too.

For weeks I received gifts almost daily from people I didn't know. They handmade jewelry, rosaries, and other sweet presents in blue, Fofi's favorite color. Someone even offered to do bracelets with an angel to sell in school. Every student seemed to be wearing a Fofi bracelet to help keep her memory alive. The ultimate present was that she would always be remembered.

After 33 years and a broken heart, I finally understood a lesson my parents had been teaching me my entire life: we must invest time, talent, and treasure to live in community with people who share our core values. I didn't need the money, food or gifts that my community offered. I also had enough support from my family and friends. What they gave me—that I unknowingly needed most of all—was hope.

My daughter's death was the death of my life as I knew it. It was the homicide of my dreams and my unborn grandchildren. For a long time, it felt like the end of my joy and smile. The 'I' I had known was gone, along with the hope of ever getting that "me" back.

I felt hopeless.

Though I am a woman of faith, hope was hard to reach during that time. It was blocked by heavy loads of darkness and pain. Mutilating thoughts prowling in my mind obstructed the way. But hope found a way to peak in every chance it got. It shone bright in the hearts of others. Every hug, prayer, card, text, email, message, phone call, and bite of the home-cooked dinners shone the light of hope for me. Their compassion and kindness towards me served as an oxygen mask when I was gasping for air.

Looking back, I did have something to be grateful for, not only on the first Thanksgiving after the loss of Fofi, but for the rest of my life. I am forever thankful for my community and for my dad, who taught me how to build that village through his example. I am grateful for the painful memories that have taught me invaluable lessons. I also appreciate learning that I can be the face of God to others by simply being *there* when it's hard to stick around.

Thanksgiving came and went, but my gratitude for the pain and the people who helped through it, remains.

CHAPTER 10

Fofi's Third Birthday

Hope usually followed my somber days. I learned to expect it. Ever since that glorious day in St. Augustine, I often sought hope in the form of rainbows. They uplifted me as if it was Fofi herself making an appearance.

I once read that a rainbow is the bridge between Heaven and Earth. They represent God's promise that there will be calm after the storm and are a symbol of hope.

I also learned that babies born after the loss of a child are called "rainbow babies." I could understand why. The baby in my womb brought us immense joy and the hope that we could be happy again. She did not replace the void Fofi left in our hearts, but she *was* a reminder of God's promise.

Although my spirit was longing for signs of hope, people felt compelled to tell me all the horrible things that were happening around us. "This child was diagnosed with cancer… That parent died and left three little kids behind…So-and-so is going through adversity alone and is severely depressed…A teenager died in an accident…," I couldn't stand it. I was hypersensitive to others' pain and I had enough with my own.

I did my best to disconnect when I heard sad news. It was hard not to care though. I knew all too well how cruel it felt to see the world go on while mine had stopped. I also understood how far a random act of kindness from a stranger could go. These thoughts of empathy prevented me from ignoring the misfortunes of the outside world.

Fofi's spirit also impeded my attempts to look the other way. As her third birthday approached—three months after her passing—I asked her time and time again, "Fofi, what do you want for your birthday?" I tried coming up with ideas, but none seemed right. *Maybe I should do a video of her life and have the family come to watch it. But wait, what if I'm not in the mood to see anyone and then I'm stuck with people in my house? Who was I kidding? Everyone will want to come. That would be overwhelming. Forget the video.*

Six weeks before her birthday, I finally got it. I would offer a Mass. It was the perfect way to celebrate her life. The icing on the cake was that after an hour I would be free to go if I felt vulnerable or needed time alone. I got so easily overwhelmed those days that I dreaded being stuck with social responsibilities. I called the church and reserved the date. As usual, they were kind and accommodating. *Phew! One less thing to worry about. Wait, but what does Fofi want for her birthday?*

FOFI'S THIRD BIRTHDAY

I am very particular about presents. I will often be the one who shows up at birthday parties without holding a gift. On the one hand, I sometimes fail to plan ahead. On the other, I dislike buying things that end up being returned or regifted. Instead, I schedule dates to treat my birthday friend or wait until I find the perfect something for that person. Then, randomly, I show up with a months-belated birthday present that I know will bring a smile to my loved one.

I wanted a meaningful gift for Fofi and, this time, I was committed to having it ready on time. I continued to ask, *what do you want, my sweet Fofi?* The answer came unexpectedly at the conclusion of a client therapy session. She looked at me and said, "Betsy, your story and unwavering faith have inspired me profoundly. You should start a foundation in your daughter's honor so you can reach and inspire many more people."

"Whoa! No way! I've got too much on my plate to add anything more. I can't!" I said.

"You have a lot of people that love and support you. You wouldn't have to do it alone," she insisted, planting the seed.

That idea haunted me for the rest of the day and week. *Ughhhh... Seriously, Fofi? That's what you want?* I prayed for confirmation and it came in the form of peace. That's how God speaks to me; through peacefulness. I can be hard-headed, but when God places a petition in my heart, I obey. *Okaaaay*, I thought to myself begrudgingly.

Content with my confirmation, I was committed. I would start a foundation to honor Fofi. I figured that would also take care of my fervent desire to keep her memory alive. But what was the foundation going to be about? Again, I submitted to prayer. Who do you want to serve, Fofi? Lord, please guide me through this.

Two weeks went by with no answer. Her birthday was just a month away at this point. One night, I stayed up late cleaning the kitchen. Everyone slept while I swept the floor.

I found myself thinking about Fofi's kind heart. Although she was only two, she understood compassion.

My best friend's son was Fofi's age and couldn't walk yet due to his condition of cerebral palsy. Whenever other children came to our house, everyone ran to the playground or jumped on the trampoline, but when he came, we set up a blanket for him to sit on. Noticing that he couldn't move with the same ease as her other friends, Fofi chose to play with him while others had fun in our backyard. Fofi couldn't stand seeing someone excluded. She also didn't do well with witnessing sadness in children.

I remembered a day in which Fofi and I were at a birthday party, dancing in front of each other, holding hands. She suddenly stopped moving, let go of my hands, and walked away from me. Confused, I turned around to ask where she was going. Next, I saw her hug a younger girl who was crying. I just stood there, delighted.

"It's okay, don't cry. It's okay," she told the little one to console her while she embraced her.

Fofi had the virtue of mercy. She had the ability to see individuals that felt invisible. She brought hope to those who endured some form of pain.

That's it! I thought to myself with the broom in hand. *The foundation will serve children she typically felt drawn to care for—those having experienced some sort of misfortune.* At that moment it became clear to me that's what she wanted. Inspired by the revelation, I immediately wrote some notes on my phone and went to sleep with a profound sense of relief.

Having just one month left and being the woman of action that I am, I started working on my daughter's birthday gift first thing the next morning. I reached out to a friend who did websites, one who's an attorney that could help with the legalities of creating a non-profit, and an adoptive uncle, who could help with the logo as a graphics designer. I was humbled by their desire and disposition to offer their time and expertise free of charge. My client had been right. I didn't have to do this alone.

I sat down to write the website (LaFofisRainbow.org) content in the very same walk-in closet where I hid two months prior. As I typed, I cried and wished I were writing a birthday card instead of the description of a foundation that would only come to existence because she had died. Although it felt right, it was painful.

In tears, I called Father Miguel (The other pastor at St. Timothy) to reserve Fofi's birthday Mass and asked if I could present the foundation to the community. He was compassionate and accommodating. Realizing how upset I was, he also reminded me that I didn't have to do this right now. That's when he first noticed the pressure I put on myself to be perfect, something I didn't understand until years later. He became one of my "therapists" and my spiritual leader throughout my journey, during which I learned a lot more about God and myself than I anticipated.

Everything fell into place effortlessly. December 3rd, 2013 arrived, and I was ready to celebrate my daughter's 3rd birthday. I spent all day preparing for the introduction of Fofi's Rainbow Foundation to the community.

Suddenly, a thought came to my mind. *To think that I was going to wait for her princess celebration.* I planned on hiring Princess Jasmine for Fofi's birthday that year. She was obsessed with the Disney movie Aladdin. A month before her passing, I felt an urge to get her the princess beforehand. I was afraid that by December she wouldn't be as crazy about Jasmine as she was during that time, and I really wanted to give her that joy.

I grew up in a very practical home. Birthdays were not a big deal and my parents never really celebrated them with parties or special activities. This didn't go well with my dreamy self, so when I created my own family, I went above and beyond to make my loved ones feel extra special during their birthdays and every day.

Not caring about how expensive and unreasonable it was to hire a princess for no special occasion, I planned a princess party for Fofi and hired Jasmine. Ironically, the reason for this gathering was the very activity that took her life. I promised Fofi that if she passed to the next level in her swimming classes (I knew this was a possibility), I would call the princess to come to the house that Thursday afternoon in July. When we got to swimming class, she said, "Don't worry, Mami. I am not going to be scared and I will swim really well today." She did and she passed to level four!

I kept my end of the promise and, after showering, her friends started arriving in princess dresses. Soon, Princess Jasmine showed up at the door. I can still picture her face glowing and her smile radiating. My girl enjoyed the entire hour with the princess like I've never seen any other birthday girl relish such an experience. As I write this, I close my eyes and see her dancing, while holding Princess Jasmine's hand and looking up at her face in awe.

As I sat quietly reminiscing on this, bittersweet tears left my eyes. Though I was experiencing the heartache of not having her to sing Happy Birthday to, I felt great comfort in knowing that I never waited to celebrate her in life. I had no regrets with Fofi. There was no kiss I didn't give her, no book I didn't read to her at night, and no lullaby left unsung. There was also no birthday wish left unkept.

The day of Fofi's Mass finally came. As I was getting ready, I felt compelled to communicate with Chichi about my feelings. I had done a good job of managing my emotions in front of her, but I was also mindful of sharing my grief to give Chichi permission to feel hers. I said, "Chichi, my love, if you see Mami crying today, it's because I miss Fofi." She replied, "But, Mami, you don't have to miss Fofi. She is always with you." She grabbed my hand with hers, placed them on my chest, and said confidently, "Mami, Fofi's in your heart, remember?"

My daughter's wisdom disarmed me and eased my grief. My first tears that night were not for Fofi. They were tears of joy, as I prayed that one day I could have the faith and wisdom of my four-year-old.

I arrived at church feeling anxious. After the final blessing of the Mass, Father Miguel asked me and Alain to go up to the altar. I stood there once again, behind the podium that served as a cane to hold me up three months prior. I was trembling and my heart was pounding. I don't remember exactly what I said, but I know I expressed my love for Fofi and my fervent desire to celebrate her life and continue her legacy. I wanted to keep her memory alive.

I once heard a man say he didn't fear the first death, but was terrified of the second. "Second death?" I asked. "Yes, that's when people forget you; when you didn't touch enough lives or created an impact." I couldn't save Fofi from her first death, but for as long as I shall live, I will NEVER let her memory die.

Before our loved ones, I shared a description of La Fofi's Rainbow Foundation and humbly asked for support. The organization wasn't about giving money, but rather the gift of time and talent to bring hope to those going through hopeless situations. It was beautiful to see how many people were willing to give of themselves to help others in Fofi's name. To this day, my heart continues to be full of gratitude toward them.

That night, we left the church and my friends gave out hundreds of blue balloons. We released them for Fofi to play with in Heaven. I was looking up at the sky filled with blue dots, when Chichi tugged on my skirt.

"Did we really have to give alllll the balloons to Fofi? She complained.

I chuckled.

CHAPTER 11

Surviving The Holidays

Fofi's third birthday was just one of the many "first" important dates we would have without her. The first of everything was painful. I tried to prepare mentally for each holiday or special occasion, but even when I managed to be okay during the actual date, grief struck me days later or days prior. This is what psychologists refer to as an anniversary reaction—the individual's response to unresolved grief resulting from significant losses.

Our First Christmas Without Her

After the Thanksgiving fiasco, I was determined to enjoy my children's first Christmas without the physical presence of their middle sister. I was committed to honoring my living daughter and son—along with the little peanut that had danced her way into my womb. It was going to be a beautiful day. After all, the "reason for the season" was the birth of Baby Jesus. I wanted Him to be reborn in my broken heart—and, hopefully, mend it.

On December 25th, 2013, exactly four months after Fofi's death, I snuck out of my room quietly to get everything ready for Chichi and Gordi. I wanted them to experience the joy of going through their stockings and opening presents. I may have eaten the half cookie Santa left to sprinkle some sweetness on my day.

I was full of gratitude for my faith, the love and support by which I was surrounded, and especially the lives of the little people and handsome man I lived with. The day was magical! The smiles that radiated from my children's faces when they saw Santa's doings were priceless. Their excitement became mine. My pain was numbed by the medicine of joy that Baby Jesus delivered that Christmas in my home. I felt grateful for having the ability to appreciate what I DID have, rather than experiencing the natural tendency of focusing on what I had lost.

My kids played with their new toys. They also enjoyed the company of the grandparents, uncles, and aunties who visited with surprises. It didn't get old to witness their bliss. The evening approached and we got ready to attend Mass, as we did every 25th of the month since our daughter's passing. What a perfect way to wrap up such a wonderful day! Church was our happy place, and we felt closer to our heavenly angel during our visit.

Alain wrapped me in his arms throughout the Mass celebration. The numbing effect of the anesthetic joy faded away. I could feel the pain again. My broken heart had not mended after all. Tears rolled down my cheeks and my chest moved back and forth as if sadness was impeding me from breathing properly. My abs contracted as I crunched forward to hold inside the explosion of agonizing emotions that had taken over me.

I took a deep breath. And then another one. *Inhale peace and exhale pain*, I told myself.

I tried to get a grip on myself and concentrate on the message that the priest was sharing as part of the homily. I don't remember what he said exactly, but I have a clear image of how he said it. The tall, dark, Haitian man was full of contagious joy. His beautiful smile and white teeth never hid during the Mass. He spoke loudly and with enthusiasm. His heart exploded with ecstatic glee as he shared about the birth of Jesus.

I didn't get it. How could this man be so thrilled about Jesus being born, when he already knew the torturous crucifixion that this poor baby was going to endure? How do you celebrate life, when a painful death will follow?

I was jealous of the priest's joy. I wanted it so badly. I remember thinking, *I want to get there. I want to think of Fofi with a heart full of joy and gratitude for having enjoyed her for three years. I want to celebrate her life, rather than dwell on her death. I want to believe she's eternal and forget about this temporary thing we call life. I want her birthday to be like Christmas—a day of celebration!* But *wanting* and *getting* take time to align. This synergy is only possible through proactive work. I describe the process in Part 2 of the book.

New Year's Eve

New Year's Eve approached soon after and was particularly hard. We were visiting my home island of Puerto Rico. Growing up, I loved the Christmas holidays with my extended family. I'm really close to my aunts and uncles, and I'm obsessed with my cousins. I was excited to see everyone on the last day of the year, yet terrified that everybody but one would be there.

Five…four…three…two…one…Happy New Year!!! The joyous announcement of a new beginning caused me to react unexpectedly. I suddenly broke into tears and found myself wailing and gasping for air as 2014 stabbed me in the heart. My body plummeted, but Alain rescued me from falling on the floor. I realized that the year during which I last saw my daughter, was gone.

It was over.

Alain held me in his arms for as long as he could before my other family members asked to hug me too. One by one, my strong male cousins—and then my other family members—wept with me as they embraced me. Their love and compassion moved me. Their warmth soothed my aching heart once more and brought back hope.

That hope was reflected on my Facebook post the following night:

I am the mother of four beautiful children, including my little Fofi. I, like our Blessed Mother, said YES to God when He asked that I be the mother of Veronica. I carried her in my womb, gave birth to her and took really good care of her. I loved Fofi with all my heart and soul.

The pain I feel is not nearly as strong as the joy I feel for having been her mother. Like Mary, I am blessed and thankful. This year I will be enjoying the birth of my fourth child, for whom my little Fofi gave her life. Mia Valentina is another precious gift from God and this is her year, so I welcome 2014!

This is what life looked like those days. I went from deep despair, to moments of clarity and hope.

CHAPTER 12

A New Year

Every "first" memorable occasion from then on was bittersweet. In January, Chichi had her first school Field Day ever. Growing up, I longed for my parents to be in my school events, but their commitment to corporate jobs prevented them from attending most. I was excited to be there with my daughter.

I put the biggest gold bow on Chichi's hair and a cute tutu in the same color. I wore two ponytails myself, with a gold ribbon on each, and the field day t-shirt. I was ready!

I dropped off Chichi at school and went next door to the Blessed Sacrament, a cozy Catholic chapel in which the body of Christ is exposed for adoration. This became my happy place. It was even more peaceful than the walk-in closet where I hid and healed right after Fofi's passing. I sat there in prayer.

After about 15 minutes, I stepped outside and joined the herd of parents that waited to cheer on their children. There were over 100 people in line. I've never been fazed by crowds, but for some reason, I suddenly felt overwhelmed.

As I approached the entrance where the administration welcomed us with sign-in sheets, I started crying hysterically and couldn't control it. Tons of eyes were on me. Meanwhile, I wanted to hide under the table. I felt so ashamed. One of the teachers, who is also a family friend, saw me and immediately held me tightly in her arms. She was a lifesaver. I buried my face in her shoulders and felt safe again.

Grief struck me unannounced that day. I didn't see it coming, nor was I sure what exacerbated it. I do remember seeing other children in line with their parents and thinking that Fofi would've been there with me to cheer on her best friend. That was the bitter moment of the sweet Field Day experience.

After composing myself, I went to the races and had a blast. I may have even lost my voice during the tug of war, screaming at a bunch of cute 4-year-olds.

Valentine's Day
Valentine's Day rolled around. "Fofi" used the occasion to send Chichi and Gordi sweet gifts and a card. Alain and I left drawings, sweets, and love letters under "La Fofi tree" on her behalf. The letters said, *"You will always be my BFFs. Will you be my Valentine, Chichi? Gordi?"*

We worked hard to keep Fofi's memory alive. She was present in our daily lives and talking about her was as normal and welcomed as three meals a day. Fofi was such a part of her siblings' lives that they never thought to exclude her. As it turns out, Chichi also had a Valentine's day card for her best friend.

Her teachers helped her write it. It read, *I miss you, Fofi. You will always be my Valentine.*

Daddy's Birthday

Alain's birthday followed on April 2nd. I could tell his mood was down. He confessed to feeling particularly sad that morning. I called him throughout the day to check on him and it didn't seem to help. My heart hurt for him. I prayed he would experience feeling the first word of the birthday song: *Happy.*

He missed her so dearly. Fofi was a very loving and affectionate little girl. Had she been there, she would have given Daddy tons of hugs and kisses that would've lasted all day.

Alain is not one to dwell on pain or engage in pity parties. Although he allows himself to feel, he is good about redirecting that pain and changing his focus after a little while. This time, it didn't come that easy for him, so he went for an approach that never fails. He chose to make it about someone else that day.

Alain is a man of simple, yet thoughtful gestures. He shifted his sadness to the joy of bringing a smile to another person. He went to visit a friend whose wife had recently given birth to a baby boy. The joy his friend experienced with the surprise visit overpowered the grief that had clouded his day. He was a new man when he got home, and my birthday wish for him was fulfilled.

Our Easter Resurrection

After Alain's birthday, we celebrated Easter; but we all know there is no Resurrection without death. On Good Friday—the day Christians commemorate the crucifixion of Jesus—I felt the darkness of that somber moment we still remember 20 centuries later. For the first time in my life, I truly understood the meaning of this day, which is such a big part of my faith.

I could feel Mary's pain, as I imagined what she must've endured witnessing her son die so tragically. I wished so badly that she would have written a book about her experience. I wanted to cope with my grief the way she dealt with hers, with unwavering faith and intact grace.

I'm sure Mary knew a truth I learned through my loss: love transcends time and space. We never have to lose the people who died. We can learn to relate to them at a spiritual level. To love my daughter and feel her presence, she didn't have to be here after all. Similarly, I've never had to see God physically to worship and love Him dearly.

On Easter Sunday, we gathered to celebrate at my in-law's house. As usual, we had a delectable brunch, a fun egg hunt, and a real-life Easter bunny. The day was peaceful. I felt prepared for this holy-day, maybe because I had already faced the darkness of my very own Good Friday two days prior. Easter was a reminder that just as the cross was the path to life, grieving is the way to healing.

Mother's Day Gift of Life

After experiencing so much anguish in previous holidays, I prepared mentally for Mother's Day and found some relief during this special occasion. I felt more happiness than sadness. I rejoiced in the gifts of love I received from my family, including the bundle of joy that couldn't wait to exit my womb. Mia Valentina, my youngest, was due in May, the month we celebrate Mother's Day.

As one of my gifts, Alain made the kids record a video for me. He also managed to include one in which Fofi said, "Mami, yo te amo," or "Mommy, I love you." Alain is not technology savvy, so the thoughtfulness of this present made it even more special. Besides, I didn't have many pictures or videos of me with the kids. Alain and I joke about how our children may grow up thinking they had an absent mother because I'm nowhere to be found in old photos. The truth is that I'm always the one behind the lens. I just hope they remember I was there!

Mother's Day came and went uneventfully. The crisis came two days later, when I attended my doctor's appointment. I saw my obstetrician's colleague, who recommended that I tie my tubes the day of Mia's birth. He explained that my three consecutive C-sections contributed to the weakening of my uterus and having more children would put me in danger.

What? You want me to grieve the end of motherhood the very day I'm supposed to celebrate it? The thought of becoming sterile was dreadful to me. It was precisely my ability to have another baby that saved me from despair. Mia had brought joy to my life at a time when all I knew was pain.

I also remembered a thought Alain had shared in the early conversations of our grief. He explained that a part of him felt that our loss was like a consequence for us trying to "play God" by deciding to get a vasectomy. I know this sounds irrational, but when the doctor told me to tie my tubes, I thought: *What if I cause the death of another one of my children by making the same mistake?* I understood conceptually that God wouldn't do such a thing, but my battle with grief, guilt, and unanswered questions clouded my reason.

I left the doctor's office deflated. I cried all the way home. Fear took hold of my entire body. *What am I going to do?* Intrusive thoughts entered my mind. *What if we lost another child and then I couldn't procreate and be happy again?*

I connected fertility to hope in those days. Learning about my pregnancy was the one thing that brought some joy during my deepest pain. I didn't want to destroy fecundity the same day I co-created life with God.

I didn't have to.

On my next appointment, my obstetrician decided for me. "Betsy, even if you asked me, I wouldn't tie your tubes. I've seen your uterus three other times and I assure you I will keep you safe." Dr. Albert Triana was my angel. He had been empathetic and supportive during my loss and throughout my pregnancy. He was well aware of my physical health, but he also understood my heart. I felt peace.

Then another thought haunted me. *What if I'm not able to fully rejoice the day of Mia's birth, as I did with her three siblings?* I feared grieving Fofi instead of celebrating Mia. I dreaded focusing on the death that made her birth possible. Had Fofi not died, we would've gone through with the vasectomy and there would be no Mia.

I wanted to delight in the birth of her life, so I prayed faithfully. I asked God to let me enjoy that moment. I visualized myself feeling peaceful and joyous that day. I imagined her angelic face and smiled. I used my fear to prepare. I was determined to not let it ruin the birth of my rainbow baby.

At 37 weeks of pregnancy—on May 19, 2014—I woke up realizing that Mia hadn't moved in my womb all night. Per doctor's orders, I prepared to go in for a sonogram. I sat on the floor of my master bathroom to pray. I felt scared. I was so fearful of losing her. I begged God to take care of my daughter, but then I remembered the last time I implored him to keep my child safe.

I became angry. *Why pray? He's gonna do whatever the heck He wants anyway.* I questioned the power of prayer. I wondered whether it was a waste of time to try to convince the all sovereign God of doing what *I* wanted.

I called my mom. She always seems to have the answers to my spiritual questions.

I didn't even greet her when she answered. "Mami, why should I pray if God is going to do whatever He wants in the end?" She reminded me we don't pray to convince God of anything. "Prayer doesn't change God's mind, Betsy. It changes YOU. It soothes your grieving heart and calms your fears. Prayer also gives God permission to intervene, if He feels it's in your best interest."

I understood once again that prayer is the way through which we grant God the access to our lives and surrender our struggles to Him. It's how we put Him in command and agree to His guidance.

I prayed again. *Lord, please take care of my baby. I beg you to keep her safe and healthy. You know how much I already love her. Please grant me the blessing to have her, raise her, love her, guide her. Let her be fine and help me deliver her safely, God, pleeeease!*

The sonogram confirmed that something was wrong. Mia's heart and movement had slowed down. She had to come out immediately.

I prayed some more. *God, I'm leaving you in charge. Please give me peace and the faith to trust your will.*

I rushed to the hospital three days before my scheduled wax appointment, with no manicure, no hair done, and without a bag. Nothing mattered. I was excited. All I could think about was that I was going to meet my ray of sunshine that very day.

As I laid on the stretcher, a pleasant thought crossed my mind: *Wow, I'm not scared anymore. The prayers worked!*

A couple of hours later, I was holding my precious, blue-eyed baby girl in my arms. At that instant, all my fears disappeared. My dream came true. I was ecstatic with the birth of my princess. I thought of Fofi, but with a smile on my face. I imagined how overjoyed she was from heaven. Mia's birth was perfect.

Father's Day

Although Mia was also the perfect Father's Day gift for Alain, I still continued our annual tradition. Every year, since Chichi was born, I created a Father's Day movie in which I featured all the pictures and videos we had taken the previous year with Alain and the kids. I included meaningful songs, the children's voices, and special memories. It usually took me over 40 hours to complete this project. This year, the hours seemed endless as I relived every moment we spent with Fofi during her last days of life. The cruel reality of being robbed of her radiance, as evidenced by her absence in the latter footage, destroyed me.

I started the video with Fofi and ended it without her. This crushed my heart. I carried on regardless. I really wanted to give Alain and our children this gift of memories. I embraced the pain and buckled up for the ride.

There was bitterness in every sweet moment of that video editing. Every smile and sense of tenderness towards a memory was followed by tears, wailing, and heartache. But God gave me the strength to push through.

Hours before Father's Day arrived—while everyone at the house slept—I finally completed my project. I wrote a message to Alain at the end of the video. In it, I acknowledged our loss, but I emphasized our blessings.

It was clear from that movie of our previous year that we didn't just survive those months. We truly and fully lived them. We laughed with our other children, took them to places, and cared for them with immense love. We also welcomed our rainbow bundle of joy with open arms, and continued to show up for our family, friends, and community.

If strangers watched that video, they would never know how much pain was consuming our insides. How was this possible? Even though we were not capable of seeing them while they were happening, we truly had joyful moments. That's what pain does with its intensity; it conceals the joy. It blinds us.

However, just because we don't focus on the blessings, doesn't mean that they're not there.

As I reflected and stared at the computer, I thought to myself, *when our kids are older and can understand the pain that we endured, they will watch this Father's Day movie and know that we loved them.* Hopefully, they will also see why Mommy and Daddy have such deep faith. There was no other way, but through the grace of God, that we could have lived so fully during those first months.

Alain was not expecting the video this year. Besides not seeing me work on it, he told me not to worry about it. He imagined how painful it would be for me, and I suspect he was also resisting watching it himself.

On Father's Day morning, the kids and I gave him a gift and homemade cards. Right when he thought we were done, we surprised him with the movie. The look on his face suggested conflicting emotions. Was he excited or nervous? He smiled anyway.

Alain sat on the family room couch while I put on the video. Chichi, who is crazy about her dad, threw herself on top of him and got comfortable in his arms. I held Mia on my lap and had Gordi lean on me. We pressed play and the DVD I had burnt hours prior started showing images and sounds we were familiar with. We fixed our eyes on the big screen.

Soon, our eyes filled with tears. The kids, however, were oblivious to the mixed thoughts and emotions in their parents' minds. They were as happy as can be. They loved watching themselves and enjoyed reliving the fun memories we experienced as a family. I grew accustomed to the bittersweet nature of moments that were once perfect, but this time there was definitely more sweet than bitter. At that instant, all the pain of doing the video was worth it.

That feeling of accomplishment was rare in those days. During my grief, I was often in the mood of doing nothing. Actually, I did feel like crying, sleeping, and being left alone. My body was always tired, my mind drained, and my spirit low. Everything I did was exhausting. I had no energy, motivation, or aspirations.

Accomplishing big goals, like a 40-hour project that triggered powerful emotions, was 10 times more challenging than when I was not grieving. But you know what I realized when I finished watching that video with my family? I had been succeeding way more than I had given myself credit for. I fulfilled some basic, yet difficult goals every day since my Fofi's death.

I got out of bed when it was easier to remain laying down. I smiled at my kids when my heart was crying. I cooked, bathed, fed, cared for, and nurtured my family when I needed to be cared for myself. I had gone on dates and made love to my husband when my desires were null. I had accompanied my clients in their pain, while sometimes reliving my own.

I may not have done everything to my usual standards, but I had showed up to the best of my ability. I understand now that when you're in pain, your 100% feels like a 50% to you, but it is still your best, and that is an accomplishment. With that Father's Day movie, I realized that my feeling of fulfillment wasn't because of putting together the video, but because my 50% best effort showed, and it made the difference in our lives.

Progress, Not Perfection

With this, and many similar experiences, I started focusing on progress, not perfection. I learned to be okay with 50% when that was all I had to give. I also understood that with time and effort 50 turns into 60 and 70, but I could revert to 50 at any given moment. Progress is not linear.

There were times in which I handled situations, holidays, and triggers gracefully. I was astonished by my progress. At other instances, I felt like a failure who couldn't apply the simplest clinical skills to get it together. It seemed like I'd take one step forward and three steps backward.

But I wasn't retracting. I experienced it more like falling in place. When you fall, the effort you make to get up strengthens you. It builds resilience and wisdom.

One particular incident during my first year of grief reminds me of the nonlinear nature of progress. Shortly after Fofi passed, Alain told me that he was amazed at how gracefully I was responding to my pain.

Seven months later, we went on a date to the Miami Open, an international tennis tournament that used to take place in Key Biscayne. We ate delicious food and had a lovely evening watching an incredible game with famed tennis player Roger Federer. The first time we went to this event together we were dating, so when the game ended, we walked around reminiscing and feeling very romantic. It was a beautiful night.

As we headed towards the parking lot, something triggered me. I don't remember exactly what it was. It may have been a child, a tree, a thought, or anything that reminded me of Fofi. It could have even been the joy that I felt at that moment. Grief in those days wouldn't let me fully enjoy a sweet moment.

We got into the car and Alain gently held my left hand as we drove off. Tears started streaming down my cheeks. I looked outside the window of the passenger seat to hide my pain from Alain. I often struggled with feeling like a "Debbie Downer," so I tried to hide my emotions in moments like these to not ruin them. Sad thoughts persisted, despite my attempt to control them.

A NEW YEAR

Soon the tears became sobs and Alain noticed. He seemed confused. We had such a lovely outing. He looked at me and, with honesty, confessed softly, "Do you remember when I told you I was impressed with how well you were handling our loss?" I nodded, and he continued, "I take it back." *Seriously? Did this guy really just say that?* I looked up at him, searching for a sign that revealed he was joking, but the look on his face told me otherwise.

I felt a rush of anger blast off like a rocket from the pit of my stomach to my face, causing my cheeks to redden. Right before I opened my mouth to fight back, I caught myself. I took a deep breath and acknowledged the innocence in his gaze. He had no intention to offend and was oblivious as to how much his comment hurt.

Fortunately, my many years of clinical training saved me from ruining the night. I knew that it was my interpretation of what he said that really hurt, not his actual words. In my mind his comment sounded more like, "I admired your strength, but now I realize you're just a wimp. You are a disappointment." Rationally, I knew this to be false. Alain loved and admired me unconditionally. He had a history of not being the most tactful person, so saying what came to mind was not odd. He also felt safe telling me anything because I had become great at not taking things personally.

Nowadays I think of that memory and can't help but giggle. This morning, as I started writing this section, I reminded Alain about this incident and his evil smirk suggested how far he's come along in becoming one of the most validating and empathetic men I know. He couldn't believe he said such a thing! That's the beauty of all the undesirable situations we endure in life. We learn and grow from them until they become a great story one day.

Grief Is Not Linear

My story with Alain illustrates that grief is not linear. You don't go from one stage of grief to the next one in order, nor do you increasingly become graceful without having setbacks. You can also go from having the night of your life to sobbing uncontrollably at the drop of a hat, or vice versa. Grief is unpredictable, and it is unique to each individual.

There is no "correct" way of grieving or assigned length of time allocated to the pain of loss. That day of the tennis tournament, my husband thought that after seven months I should have been less reactive to random triggers. Or maybe he figured that since I had so many "good" days, returning to a moment of crisis was a setback or sign of pathology. It wasn't. It was just me grieving the way I knew how.

My Birthday

The last special date before the first anniversary of my Fofi's death was my 35th birthday, on July 19th. I could say that it was the worst birthday of my life, as I expected, but the truth is that it may have been one of the best.

My parents came from Daytona a day early to be with me. Then at night, two of my favorite cousins flew in from Maryland and gave me the best surprise ever! One of them lived in Vietnam, so I hadn't seen her in years. It was overwhelmingly beautiful to feel her embrace and listen to all the unspoken words she told me during that hug. I heard her silence say, "I love you, cousin. My heart has been with you during this painful year."

Alain stood behind with his pleased smile and touched my heart with his thoughtfulness. He had driven an hour to pick them up from the Fort Lauderdale Airport. He also brought with him my favorite dessert: the mascarpone cheesecake from Il Gabbiano in Downtown Miami. What a way to start my birthday celebration a night early!

My two cousins slept over at my house. The sleepover reminded me of the good old days when we were neighbors in Puerto Rico and did pajama parties at each other's homes. We reminisced and giggled like the little girls we once were. I was so happy we were together.

It was still the day before my birthday, and it was already wonderful. Both of my cousins had their own families, so taking time away from them to be with me made me feel special. I was so excited that I struggled to fall asleep.

My day arrived and I woke up to a lovely, sunny day with a smile on my face. I sprung out of bed to greet my guests and give my little ones their morning squeeze. They had handmade beautiful cards and recorded the cutest birthday video. I enjoyed continuous surprises planned by my husband throughout the day.

We went out to dinner that evening with my cousins, siblings-in-law, and best friends. It was the most fun birthday dinner I've ever been to. Having people I love dearly celebrate my life was nice, but experiencing genuine joy after so much pain made it exceptional.

After dreading the unpleasant emotions, I thought the day would bring, I felt relieved with how much better reality was than I anticipated. I had worked diligently on changing my focus from what I was missing to what I still had. My efforts finally paid off…until a few days later.

When my family left, I cried and cried. Grief always caught up to me. Even when I managed to prepare and navigate the special date smoothly, I broke down afterwards. Free of distractions, a moment of stillness would pull me back into the pain of missing my daughter.

CHAPTER 13

The First Anniversary

A month later, I didn't think I could bear the first anniversary of Fofi's death. I imagined I'd experience emotions that would put me on my knees as that first night I found myself deranged, rocking back and forth on a bathroom floor. The anticipatory fear creeped in again.

My grief was still raw after a year. It was too difficult to look for the silver lining. Obstacles made up of painful thoughts, flashbacks, nostalgia, and heartache prevented me from seeing the light. Pushing through was overwhelming.

Staying "positive" seemed impossible. In my mind, I knew I could, but my heart was too fragile to be consistent in its attempts. I had moments of clarity and optimism, but they depleted my energy. It was exhausting to focus on blessings when the memory of my loss was constantly knocking at my door.

I sought out support by asking my parents to come stay with me. I wanted them close during the dreaded day of the one year anniversary. A part of me feared that day would be a mental and emotional recreation of my *Good Friday*—the day I felt crucified with the death of my daughter. If that was to be the case, I wanted my parents with me this time. I wanted to be held in their arms and have their shoulders to cry on.

The anticipated suffering arrived early and unexpectedly. I hadn't prepared for Chichi's first day of kindergarten. That day I woke up excited to make it special for her. I had the perfect hairdo in mind and the most beautiful bow to match it. I did her hair, while her daddy prepared a delicious, healthy breakfast that would prevent her from having a rumbly tummy at school. We took some pictures of her alone and then with the family, holding a sign that read *First Day of Kindergarten.*

Suddenly, I reviewed the pictures and felt the family photos seemed incomplete. Fofi was missing. She had participated in the bow selection the previous year. It had been an important day because her sister was going away all day for the first time in their lives. They were partners and best friends. They had a heartwarming and unique bond. Chichi going away to school was an important milestone for Fofi too.

As I stared at the incomplete family picture on my phone, I realized that this would've been Fofi's first day of school too. It struck me that I would never leave my little princess in a classroom for the first, second, or third time. A knot formed in my stomach and traveled quickly to my throat, making breathing harder. I did everything in my power to keep smiling for Chichi and waited to be in the car before letting my tears come out. I tapped them dry and held Alain's hand until we arrived at school.

I composed myself and tried to be present and joyful for my big girl's first day. She was excited, but still got a bit emotional when it was time for Alain and I to leave. Her glossy eyes touched my heart and reminded me of last year's first day. Fofi was the one who struggled the most with Chichi staying in school. Her words echoed in my ear, "I don't want to leave. I want to stay with you, Chichi." I shared her thoughts a year later. I didn't want to go. I then remembered Chichi's reply to her sister, "But, Fofi, you can't stay here with me, so give me lots of kisses." I followed her guidance and kissed my daughter goodbye. I walked away containing an explosion of emotions that bombarded my insides.

I may have cried during the entire school day. When it was time to leave my house to pick up Chichi, I had a flashback to a year prior, when Fofi woke up early from her nap to make sure she went with me. She wanted to see her sister first.

I can still picture the embrace Fofi gave Chichi when she came out of the classroom. She jumped for Chichi to carry her and wrapped her arms and legs around her. It was as if they hadn't seen each other in a year! This time it truly had been a year.

Having cried all day helped me release the pain. I guess that's why William Young says you should never "discount the wonder of your tears" because "they can be healing waters and a stream of joy." I felt happy when I saw that the morning glossy eyes were now sparkling. Chichi loved her first day of kindergarten. Though painful, the day was officially a success.

The Healing Bank Account

Grieving is part of the process of healing. Whenever I found myself hurting more than what was usual to me, I felt I got extra credits in my healing bank account. In fact, I came up with an analogy that helps me view pain in a special way.

I believe that grief is like coins in a piggy bank. When you insert your first coin, it travels a long distance and hits the ceramic floor of the piggy bank hard. Then, as you continue to deposit coins, they accumulate and form a cushion that eases the fall and decreases the length of time during which a new coin travels to the bottom.

The same holds true for the uncomfortable emotions that characterize our mourning. With every tear, or other unique expression of grief, a cushion of hope forms. We become familiar with the pain that originally felt unbearable and learn how to embrace it, rather than escape it. The more we allow ourselves to feel that pain, the less pain we will have left to feel.

One day, we will be triggered by a memory or event that will cause a tear to slide down our face as a coin in a piggy bank. At that time, the pain will be more subtle and short lived because the piggy bank will be full of old expressions of pain that broke the fall. The old pain will diminish the new pain, while it forms a new and wiser you.

Each teardrop represents a memory, a lesson, a frame of reference. Their accumulation builds our resilience and helps us navigate new pain.

Maybe that's what happened on August 25, 2014, the first anniversary of Fofi's "angelhood". A year of pain must've created some "cushion" that relieved a bit of the heartache I anticipated. I felt prepared for this day. My parents were with me, my husband and I took the day off, and I cried all my tears days prior, like on Chichi's first day of school. I was ready to live and feel my emotions.

That day, I felt more peace than I imagined possible. We had no special plans, except to go to church at 8 a.m. after dropping off Chichi at school. I loved going to that Mass. It was cozy, quiet, and intimate. Very few people attended, so I felt I had permission to cry without worrying about who was watching. I did cry, but I found comfort in Alain's embrace and being in the presence of my heavenly Father. I felt peace despite the tug at my heart.

After Mass, we went straight to the cemetery. That became our tradition in the upcoming years. We didn't visit the cemetery often. I've always understood that Fofi is not there, so I don't usually feel the urge to go to her grave. I did, however, enjoy my visit this particular day. I was fully present. I mindfully took in the beauty of nature, the sky, the sun, the trees, and her tombstone. I read and reread her inscription:

"You are a ray of sunshine who has always illuminated us with her resplendent gaze and smile. Your charisma, wittiness, kindheartedness, and unconditional love inspire us to live like you, so that we may join you one day. You are eternal, Fofi. Let us continue feeling your sweet and loving caresses in our hearts. We love you."

That day, there was a wooden stick across the inscription, blocking one of the angels decorating the stone. It was holding a newly planted tree and I was bothered by the invasion of territory. How dare they seize space and block my daughter's angel?

Suddenly Alain said, "Baby, did you notice that tree they just planted is a royal poinciana? When it grows it will give beautiful shade to Fofi's grave. How perfect that they planted it right here!"

A Change In Perspective

Alain knows how much I love royal poincianas because they remind me of my native island, Puerto Rico. When they bloom, they give beautiful red, orange, yellow or purple flowers that adorn every single branch. They're like a giant flower bouquet.

Alain redirected my focus and changed my perspective on the irritating wooden stick. I was so bothered by the intrusion, that I didn't even notice it was holding a *flamboyan*, as we call the tree in my country. Visualizing the flowery umbrella over Fofi's grave helped me reframe the wooden stick as the one who supported my shade and adorned my daughter's backyard.

Reframing changes a negative perspective into a positive one. It also communicates to your subconscious mind that what seemed an inconvenience is truly a blessing. This results in more pleasant emotions and an elevated mood. It's such a powerful tool that I can't wait to share more about how it's transformed my life in Chapter 15.

After making peace with the wood holding the newly planted tree in place, Alain and I threw ourselves on the grass and stared at the blue, cloudless sky. *Blue was her favorite color*, I thought to myself. I noticed a short-lived breeze that caressed my face.

My eyes squinted behind my sunglasses as they faced the beaming sun that lit up the cemetery and caused drops of sweat to form in my forehead. There—kneeling on the ground—Alain and I prayed together.

There was a moment in which my heartache peeked in, but it felt different from other times. I didn't feel alone in my pain. Yes, Alain was with me, but I felt accompanied by all the men and women that wept for those buried in the surrounding graves. I was feeling my grief alongside everyone who ever lost a loved one. I was one with a whole universe of brave people that sat with their pain and welcomed it courageously, as did I at that instant.

Alain and I went home. I later spent some quality time with my parents, away from the house. I can't recall where we went, but I remember rushing back home because Alain asked me to have a minute of silence at 5 p.m., which was around the time the accident took place a year prior. I wasn't sure what to expect from that, but I wanted to honor his request.

I arrived at the house a couple of minutes late, worrying that I'd let him down. I jumped out of the car and into the house, only to see through the large family room windows that Alain was in the backyard. He was sitting on a chair in front of the pool—the same body of water that had drowned the life of my precious daughter 12 months earlier.

My heart sank. *Oh, it's that kind of silent minute, huh?* I felt scared. I had learned how to be with my pain, but I wasn't sure I knew how to help Alain through his. He had been so strong and faithful all along. He was my rock.

He always managed to overcome the unpleasant emotions of his grief by giving in to humor or simply choosing to change his focus and reframe. But there he was now—lamenting and surrendering his power to the murderer of our life as we knew it. At least that's what I thought.

THE FIRST ANNIVERSARY

Count Your Blessings

I took a deep breath and rushed outside. He pulled out a chair for me, dragged it close to his, and signaled with his hands, asking me to join him. I sat down and waited nervously.

"Baby, let's have a minute of silence for our daughter," he said. He held my right hand, closed his eyes, and said nothing. I followed anxiously.

A minute or so passed, and he began, "There is something I'd like to do with you today. It has been a year since we experienced death in our hearts, but we've made it, Baby. We are alive, together, and whole. This year has been painful, but it has also been so blessed. I'd like to take a moment to acknowledge every blessing we've had in the last 12 months."

It took me a moment to process what he was saying, but my body understood it instantly. My hunched shoulders suddenly lifted along with my gaze, which had been focused on the cream and beige pavers that once held my Fofi's lifeless body.

I looked at him in the eye trying to get some answers. I was confused. I asked telepathically, *wasn't this supposed to be a sad moment? How could we talk about blessings in the very scene we saw our daughter's life leave her body?*

Alain's eyes didn't waver. They backed up his words and silently reassured me with their glow and confidence: *Yes, Betsy. Right here—where your heart broke into pieces—we will mend it. We will sew it back together with patches of blessings.* "Ok," I finally responded convinced.

"We had Mia," Alain began.

"Cheater! I wanted to say that!" I argued playfully.

"Ok then. Our marriage is stronger and more beautiful than ever. We've proven to ourselves that our faith is strong and unwavering," he added. "We have received overwhelming love and support from family, friends, and even strangers. We have been present for our children and each other." Alain squeezed my hand.

"We created La Fofi's Rainbow Foundation and are keeping Fofi's memory alive through service. We've gained new friends and community," Alain continued. We've become stronger and kinder." I sighed. Chichi has coped with her loss gracefully and continues to be a joyful girl." Alain smiled. Gordi seemed unfazed by the loss and we've loved and nurtured him fully."

"I've become more empathetic at work because I understand pain better," I confessed.

"Did I mention we had Mia this year?" Alain proceeded cheerfully, emphasizing what a blessing she had been to our lives.

It was getting late and the sun was setting. Alain acknowledged that we could go on and on talking about our blessings for hours, but it was time to prepare for dinner. We leaned in towards each other and hugged tenderly. I felt safe in his arms. That was my favorite part of that day's blessings.

I stood up from my chair, felt my body lighter, and my mood elevated. It's amazing how much our bodies speak and feel. I floated to the kitchen and prepared for the lovely dinner we had as a family on that August 25, 2014. I looked at Fofi's empty chair and smiled.

I was starting to see her with my heart.

The next day my parents departed, leaving me in good spirits. My peace increased when I opened my social media and saw that I was tagged in tons of posts with people wearing blue and carrying signs that read, "Fofi Blue, Fofi Forever, We love you Fofi,..." among others. They wrote encouraging messages. Their compassion lifted me up. If they only knew how much those simple gestures meant to me. It's those little things that made the greatest difference in my healing.

In the afternoon, we waited for Chichi to come home from school and went across the street to my in-laws to plant a "Fofi tree." We had the avocado "Fofi tree" in my house, but this one was special because it was a gift from friends who went to every nursery in Homestead and Miami searching for a tree that gave blue flowers. When they finally found one, they told the owner of the nursery about my story and he promised to name it the "Fofi tree" moving forward.

After losing my daughter, I found great comfort in keeping her memory alive. When people remembered her, honored her, and spoke about her, I felt she remained. She continued to be real. That she is no longer present in this physical realm, does not mean she ceased to exist. My Fofi lives on forever.

I continue to include her in every celebration. My family and I have created new holiday traditions and rituals that help us find joy in our new reality. I talk to and about her daily. I've learned to connect with her in alternative ways. I continue to love her endlessly.

I survived the first year, but the Betsy I knew wouldn't have.. Pain changed me. Ironically, it brought me hope.

Part 2: Hope

CHAPTER 14

Before We Begin

Sharing my story in Part One granted you the opportunity to connect with your pain by reading about mine. Thank you for sitting in the dark with me.

In Part Two I will help you turn on the light by showing you how I made mine shine again. More than sharing my story, the focus of this section is on taking action to heal and rise above your pain. Combining my background in clinical psychology with my personal experience and unwavering faith enabled me to develop the most powerful approach to convert hurt into hope.

I will teach you the clinical and spiritual tools that have transformed my life and that of the people I serve. These will help you navigate through your struggles, while becoming the better version of yourself that God created you to be.

I have a rule I live by in my private practice and speaking engagements: my clients must leave better than they came in. I may not have instant answers or solutions to their problems, but I will always have hope to give.

And HOPE changes everything.

Hope is trusting that things will get better, even when we can't even imagine that possibility. It keeps us breathing during times of adversity. It is what helps us get up and try again and again when we collapse.

Hope brings back joy when it seems to have left forever. I pray God lets me show you the way to hope, so you may find joy, as I have.

CHAPTER 15

The Five Pillars of Healing

"Betsy, how did you go from such agonizing pain to the joy you exude?" My clients began asking this question years after my daughter died. My audiences inquired about it in speaking engagements and social media. Even my friends and family wondered.

At first, I didn't know how to respond. I assumed that everyone who experienced hardship went through the same process I did. Then people started coming to me for grief therapy and I saw how stuck they were in their traumas. Many of my clients had suffered loss years prior to my daughter dying and had not found hope yet.

People all around me were suffering, and I felt compelled to do something about it. I revisited my process to discover what I had done differently than the rest. I found the answer.

I have a superpower. It's called FAITH.

A woman once asked me, "Is it because you're so Catholic that you could find joy again?" She wasn't religious, so she questioned whether she could ever find hope.

She can. The FAITH I teach transcends religion and can be developed by anyone at any time.

Faith is the ability to believe—in yourself, in others, and in the process.

The Bible says, "...faith is the assurance of things hoped for, the conviction of things not seen" (Hebrews 11:1). Faith is trusting that you can be happy again, even if you're suffering right now. It is being confident that your pain will eventually liberate you, not condemn you. Faith allows you to have hope for a better version of your life, no matter how impossible it may seem at the moment.

I had faith that I could heal and be happy again one day. In my early stages of grief, faith enabled me to seek resources that would teach me how to heal. I found plenty of books and studies that described what grief was and what I was supposed to feel during such a process. Many described the five stages of grief developed by Elisabeth Kübler-Ross, denial, bargaining, depression, anger, and acceptance.

Unfortunately, I felt that reading about what I could expect was more nerve-racking than it was helpful. It robbed me of hope. *Do I still have to go through all of these phases before I find some relief?* I thought I needed to check off those boxes before I could proactively pursue my healing and arrive at that coveted stage of acceptance.

I already knew what grief looked like. I was living it. What I wanted was not the five stages of grief, but rather the five steps to navigating and overcoming it. I desired the HOW, not the WHAT. I wanted to find a book that taught me hope, but all I found were books that explained the hurt.

I stopped looking for answers in books other people wrote, and I started writing my own. I paid attention to the clinical tools I used during my grieving and the impact they had on my journey. I explored the approaches that failed. I studied how my clients dealt with adversity and tested the methods that led them to success. Finally, I prayed for guidance.

It was in the process of doing the work, studying the tools, and turning to God, that I discovered the formula for my superpower:

- Fertilizing pain
- Acceptance
- Interpretation
- Team
- Habits

These are the secret components to a life full of hope and healing. I have implemented and validated them with hundreds of clients in private practice, workshops, and online programs. These skills have transformed the lives of people from all walks of life who are experiencing different forms of adversity. I've seen them rise above divorce, bereavement, a child's misfortune, illness, financial hardship, and legal problems. Others have used these tools to overcome a lifetime of strained relationships, depression, anxiety, and trauma.

Regardless of the nature of your pain, F.A.I.T.H. can elevate you to the highest, most joyous version of yourself. This acronym describes the set of skills I used to rise above pain. It is the answer to *how* I went from Hurt to Hope.

F.A.I.T.H. is *my* version of the five stages of grief. The greatest difference is that the emphasis is on mitigating the grief and overcoming adversity, while becoming your greatest self.

If you are ready for some hope, open your heart and pay attention to how you can apply these tools. I have *faith* that they will help you too.

CHAPTER 16

Fertilizing Pain

The first step I took in my healing journey had to do with allowing myself to feel the pain. It took challenging my limiting beliefs regarding vulnerability to do this gracefully. I used to believe that crying was a sign of weakness and grieving was unattractive.

I don't want to cry, I often thought. I didn't want to become the depressed person who was always sad and down. I figured it was a matter of time before my friends stopped wanting to be around me. Grief was already a lonely process, so I feared alienating people further. Then I understood that what I rejected was suffering, not pain.

Pain vs Suffering

I suffered the loss of my daughter when it first happened. Unable to accept her death, I fell into darkness. I engaged in haunting flashbacks, poignant thoughts, and deep hopelessness—very much like the episode I had on the bathroom floor the night of her death. That kind of pain felt unbearable. I couldn't survive it for long; at least not without losing my mind.

One of my favorite quotes is by Japanese writer Haruki Murakami. He says, "Pain is inevitable. Suffering is optional." We can't avoid pain. We feel it when we lose a person, a thing, a dream, or our life as we knew it. We even experience it when something doesn't go our way. It is inevitable.

But pain is healthy. It is like the scab on a wound. It forms to protect the skin and looks ugly when it's there, but it reminds us that healing is taking place. Pain *is* hope. When it's present, we know something is happening within to help us grow and rise above adversity.

Suffering, however, is pain *without* hope. Being hopeless in our ability to overcome the struggle keeps us stuck in the pain. It is like picking at the scab or removing it every time it forms. In doing so, we become exposed to infection and prevent the wound from healing fully.

Suffering results when we deny reality, or when we've gotten so accustomed to the pain that it becomes our lifestyle. We suffer when pain becomes the destination, rather than the route to healing. It also takes place when we resist pain or attempt to escape it.

The Brain & Pain

The brain protects us from physical pain to fulfill the role of keeping us safe. If someone touches a hot stove top, the brain immediately sends a message to the hand, so it's removed instantly from the burning surface. The brain tells the hand, "Danger! Get out of that pain-provoking situation!" and saves it from a severe burn. The mind protects us from harm by avoiding what hurts, but not everything that hurts, harms.

Our brains didn't get the memo on welcoming emotional pain in order to heal. The mind treats heartache as if we were putting our hand on the burning stove. We are wired to resist and reject it. We fear it. But the only way to overcome pain is by feeling it.

Pain hurts, but ultimately, it protects us from harm. As Napoleon Hill states, "...every heartache carries with it the seed of an equal or greater benefit." During adversity, we must outsmart our minds and allow ourselves to feel the pain. Choosing to touch the burning flame of grief, when the brain insists on avoiding it, will heal us. Escaping it will lead to suffering, which both hurts and harms.

If we escape, numb, or avoid pain—as our brains encourage us to—it will become deeper and stronger.

Feel it

Choosing to feel the pain without falling into suffering requires that we find hope in the process. Hope is all around us, waiting to be found. It's what helps us believe that pain is temporary and has a healing purpose. I found the hope that converted my suffering into pain when I attended the Emmaus retreat. That weekend I understood that my pain was the process, not the outcome.

But it was still here! I pleaded to God, *Okay, Lord. Thank you for removing the darkness, but can you also do something about this pain, please? How do I get rid of it?*

You don't. Feel it, Betsy. The words of my aunt echoed in my mind.

My mom's sister-in-law, Titi Neyda, is very close to God. She is the kind of person that radiates peace when she speaks or just by looking at you. She is wise and sweet. Titi sees straight through your skin and into your soul. The first time I learned she had this gift was when I lost my grandma at 18. She came to me after one of the novena rosaries and asked with much love, "How is your heart doing?" She saw me and my pain. It was as if God Himself spoke to me through her and came to console me.

When Fofi passed, Titi Neyda flew to Miami to accompany me. My walk-in closet, the home of many memorable breakthroughs, was the setting of her lesson. As I desperately shed tears and begged for answers, she said softly, "Welcome the pain, Betsy. Acknowledge it's there and accept it with an open heart. Don't try to resist or change it. Embrace it. Then, surrender it to God."

At the time I was clueless as to how that was going to help. I thought to myself, *Welcome pain? What am I now, a masochist?*

It sounded so ridiculous. I was trying to get rid of the hurt and her best advice was to embrace it?

I still listened because I trust her wisdom. Titi Neyda leads by example so if this worked for her, it will work for me. *Ok. Welcome pain. Don't fight it. Acknowledge it. Embrace it. Got it.*

Easier said than done. My brain did what the brain is trained to do: resist the pain. I wanted to fast forward time to skip over it. Remembering my aunt's advice, I forced myself to sit with my feelings.

I cried every day; sometimes multiple times a day. My commute time in the car made it easier for me to *feel*. In solitude and silence, I was able to connect with my ache. At times I would listen to the *I will trust you* song and a torrential downpour of tears would follow.

These crying sessions often happened on my way to work. Shortly after losing Fofi, I wondered if I could go back to my private practice. I feared that I would be apathetic to other people's grief by looking down on them or judging their pain as inferior. *Would I feel like, "Oh please, is that what you're worried about? My daughter DIED. Get over it!"*

But that wasn't the case at all.

Three weeks after Fofi passed, I returned to work and felt more compassion than I ever had before. I learned something important: The worst pain is not that of losing a child; it's the one you experience in the present moment.

Pain is pain.

Regardless of what caused it, it hurts.

Feel it.

Good days, Bad days

I don't remember how long the dark pain lasted, but I do recall that the first year after losing Fofi was particularly hard for me. There were days—even from the very beginning—that I felt strong and positive. My friend Caroline once told me that something I said the day of Fofi's celebration of life impacted her. When I stood up behind the podium, I declared with power, "I am a woman of faith." She says that my statement conveyed the certainty that I would be okay; that my faith guaranteed God had my back and would give me the strength when my humanity gave in. She didn't understand how I could have such confidence just three days after my life as I knew it crumbled.

During those days, pain was present, but so was hope. Hope made everything better. It brought me peace amidst the ache. It promised that the rainbow would shine after the storm. It made my hurt more bearable because I knew it was temporary.

Hope gets rid of permanence, or the belief that grief will last forever.

Unfortunately, hope wasn't always present, and my positivity tank often ran low. Many days I felt like the sting would never go away. *I cannot do this forever,* played in my mind on repeat.

I didn't want to live.

I was not suicidal, but I fantasized with the day I went to Heaven with Fofi.

It was hard to focus on the blessings those days. My defenses were low, and I got sick easily. Hope seemed out of reach.

One morning, while lying in bed with cold symptoms, I bawled hysterically. Caruca, our nanny who's like family, peeked in the room and reminded me, "Betsy, your baby…"

I was pregnant with Mia and she was worried that my grief would hurt my baby girl. I feared that too. I always remember that moment because, from then on, I made it a point to talk to Mia whenever I felt sad. I often whispered, "I love you, my sweet baby. Mami is ecstatic to have you. My tears have nothing to do with you. You've brought me pure joy and I will take good care of you, my angel. Mami loves you so much."

I was able to hide my pain from Chichi when she was in school, from Gordi when he was napping, but I couldn't hide it from Mia. She lived inside of me. She heard my heartache in every beat. She ate my anguish. Having Mia gave me strength. It left me with no option but to push through. Mia was my hope at that moment.

This is when I learned the power of finding something, or someone, that gives you reason to wake up and live—not just survive.

Life that first year was a constant battle between wanting to dwell in rock bottom and knowing that's not where I belonged. At times I allowed myself to feel the pain and other moments I suffered hopelessly. A part of me enjoyed being the victim. It was easy and effortless.

Grief comes accompanied by sadness, tears, fatigue, anhedonia, and hopelessness. These consume our limited energy. Choosing to smile, getting out of bed, doing things that we don't feel like doing, or having faith require hard work. It's exhausting. That's why it's so easy to fall into suffering.

Visualizing Pain

Visualizing pain as hope may help you embrace it. This technique is used to imagine something in detail to help you accomplish it. It tricks your subconscious mind into believing that the imagery is actually true, leading you to respond accordingly. Below is a powerful visualization exercise that helps you imagine pain as the path to healing.

Close your eyes.

Wait, not yet. Read the whole thing first.

FERTILIZING PAIN

Imagine you have fallen into a black hole. There is no way to get out. You look around and you feel helpless and paralyzed with fear. The hole is so far above your head that even if you tried, you could not climb out of it.

You are in pain from the fall. Your bones are broken. You are completely alone.

You start to cry.

The tears stream down your face. You can hear each drop as it hits the ground. You cry harder. The tears rush down like a waterfall. The puddle turns into a flood.

Scared, you resist. Your fear of drowning causes you to fight the water, but your body is too weak to swim. You begin to sink. Realizing that your attempts are unproductive, you surrender. You remain still.

Suddenly, you start to rise. You are floating on your tears, and they gently push you up. You are rising. Your broken bones, and helpless arms and legs rest on their own pain. The more you let the tears out, the closer you get to the top.

Finally, you see the light. You don't need your tears any longer. They've done the work they needed to do. Your bones begin to heal. You are no longer scared. Your pain has served you.

The light you see. Relief you feel. That, my friend, is hope.

Pain Is a Fertilizer

Allowing yourself to view pain as a source of hope will help you sit with it. It will elevate you. Pain is a fertilizer. It nourishes you. It helps you blossom, thrive, and grow stronger. But what are fertilizers made of? Poop! They smell bad and are gross.

Pain stinks, just like a fertilizer. It's yucky and uncomfortable. But it strengthens you.

I own a sign that says, "You don't know how strong you are until being strong is all you can do." I thought I'd die if I ever lost a child. I remember conveying this to my nail lady, who lost her son in a similar accident. Then Fofi passed and I didn't die. I wanted to, but I didn't.

Embracing pain as a fertilizer allowed me to welcome my uncomfortable feelings as temporary and healing. The discomfort of these emotions motivated me to do anything and everything in my power to get rid of them. I sought help, engaged in habits that served me, nourished my relationship with God, and looked for blessings and hope where there was despair. I succeeded sometimes and failed the others. This process of falling and getting back up to get rid of the pain, built my strength.

My grief saved me. It felt like poop, but it exercised my resilience. Pain taught me the greatest lessons of my life, which I am now passing on to you. Pain made me strong; so strong that

I often feel invincible. I have a new perspective now. I know that if I can live without my daughter, I can deal with anything that comes my way. I am powerful. And so are you.

Feel the pain and then watch yourself blossom.

Pain Is Humbling

In addition to giving perspective and strength, pain is humbling. It shreds our self-righteousness. When we become vulnerable, we are more willing to seek support. We realize we don't know it all or have everything under control. I've always struggled with asking for help. I'm more comfortable with the roles of doing and giving, but pain consumed all my energy, leaving me depleted and empty for a long time.

I learned humility when I found myself desperately looking for hope in other people. I had to "bother" friends late at night when my anger and grief were about to explode and threatened to destroy my sanity.

I also found myself kneeling before God and begging for his mercy. My relationship with Him is the most precious gift that came from my humbling pain. My trust in Him grew after losing Fofi.

We all need help to heal and succeed. Pain humbles us to seek that support. Not asking for help isn't a sign of strength and self-sufficiency. It is a symptom of insecurity or arrogance.

Thinking you "don't want to bother," often comes from the belief that you are not worthy of others' attention and effort. That is a sign of insecurity and poor self-concept. As a child of God, you are precious. You matter. You deserve help.

When the problem is not insecurity, it is often self-righteousness. Believing that you "don't need help," suggests a sense of superiority. God doesn't need our assistance because He *is* superior and all-powerful. We, humans, can always use a little help.

Other times the thought is more along the lines of, "I don't 'bother' so others don't 'bother' me." Equating help to inconvenience, prevents us from the healing power of service and thriving in community.

There are times in which the excuse for resisting help is that we are more comfortable "giving." I still struggle with this. Assuming only the role of a "giver" disguises our sense of superiority with a seemingly humble attitude of service. Service is giving to others, but sometimes what we give is the opportunity for them to serve *us*.

Pain shreds our self-righteousness. Making us vulnerable, it reminds us of our humanity and enables us to humbly ask for help.

Pain Builds Empathy

Grief also taught me empathy and made me a better version of myself. I always thought I was a good person. Witnessing the kindness with which others treated me after Fofi's accident, made me realize how far I was from my best self. I was good to whomever came my way and I was mindful of not hurting anyone. But being good is not the same as not being bad.

True kindness comes with inconvenience and I don't think I would've gone out of my way to do for others as much as people did for me. Being empathetic was my profession, but it became my way of living when I was the recipient of the most caring human love.

Pain also teaches us empathy by creating a deep understanding of what grief feels like in our core so we may feel compassion for others enduring it too. One thing is to have a sensitivity to others' pain. Another is to have experienced it so deeply that you can't help but feel the agony that others endure.

That's empathy: the ability to connect with another's pain and the willingness to sit in the dark with that person. You don't empathize with the experience. You empathize with the pain.

Pain Is the Path, Not the Destination

Pain is not the enemy. Suffering is. As Glennon Doyle shares in her book *Untamed*, "Pain is not tragic. Pain is magic... Suffering is what happens when we avoid pain and consequently miss our becoming."

Pain is the process through which we heal. It is the foundation of growth and the pathway to joy.

Pain is the homeopathic treatment that helps us overcome adversity. It is the training program that elevates us to our best self.

When we find this kind of hope in our ache, we stop resisting it or wondering when it will be over. Instead we welcome and accept it, so we may start working on overcoming it.

This is different from getting comfortable in the pain and dwelling on it. That is suffering. Suffering is accepting pain as the final destination and removing the hope of ever rising above it.

Suffering is *not* a fertilizer. It is the dead tree that gave up and stopped using its roots to absorb water and nutrients. It does not lead to growth. Suffering is *not* humbling. Assuming hopelessness as the destination prevents you from seeking help. Suffering does *not* build empathy. You are too busy wallowing in your own misery and too consumed by it to even think others exist and feel.

Suffering does not lead to healing. It is the outcome in and of itself.

To determine whether you're in pain or suffering, visit Hurt2Hope.com/FreeResources.

CHAPTER 17

Acceptance

Embracing pain minimizes the resistance that prevents us from pursuing acceptance, the ultimate goal in the five stages of grief. When we first experience a tragedy, the first thought that comes to mind is something along the lines of *This can't be happening*.

Losing a loved one, our marriage, financial freedom, our health, or our life as we knew it is traumatic. When we go through loss, our psyche needs time to adapt and come up with a battle plan to protect us.

We experience denial and resist reality. It's our mind's natural way of buying time to see how we can combat the immense pain coming our way and find a plan of action to ensure survival. This reaction is healthy at first, but when we choose to live in denial because we don't want to experience the pain and responsibility of accepting reality, we stop living.

At the beginning of my grieving process, I often stayed up after my family went to sleep to cry and scream freely. I spent hours on my computer scrolling over pictures and videos of Fofi to ease my insatiable need to see her. I couldn't believe that she was gone. I felt I was going crazy and wanted to prove to myself that she was real by confirming that she had been in my arms days, weeks, months, and years prior.

I tried to bring her back through those memories. I couldn't accept that she was gone forever, and I would no longer sing lullabies and read books to her before bedtime. I did not want to live without my daughter. I didn't think I could.

My resistance often left me angry, hopeless, and deeply saddened. Then, one morning I dragged myself to Mass and listened intently to the readings. The word acceptance spoke to me in one of the scriptures.

I had to accept her death. Continuing to resist the fact that she was gone wore out the limited energy I had left to heal. I thought I had to wait patiently for acceptance to arrive at my door.

Acceptance is not a stage you arrive at passively after experiencing denial, anger, bargaining, and depression. I would argue that acceptance is not the last phase of grief. It is the first decision you proactively make to begin your healing journey.

Acceptance comes from the Latin word *captum*, which means taking. It is the action of taking or receiving what is offered. What is given to us in times of adversity is a cruel reality.

Acceptance, then, is welcoming our reality exactly the way it is. Like most people, I resisted reality because I was afraid of the pain that acknowledging it would bring. I could not bear more than I was already experiencing. I've learned that resistance causes more damage than the actual pain. I love how Paulo Coehlo explains this in *The Alchemist:* "Fear of suffering is worse than suffering itself."

Fighting with reality amplifies our pain because it prevents us from focusing on our healing. It keeps us busy pushing back on what is, while the true problem remains untouched. In her book *Loving what is*, Byron Katie assures that "when you argue against reality, you always lose." Resisting it will not change the situation. My nightly practice of fighting reality by proving her existence with pictures didn't bring my daughter back.

While the sight of grief may seem unbearable, we possess the human capacity to overcome it. We always have the ability to cope with what we've been dealt. Only by embracing grief will we acquire the necessary training for healing. Accepting and allowing our fertilizing pain to build resilience and character in our life is the first step to rising from adversity.

Radical Acceptance

Realizing that my resistance was turning my pain into suffering, inspired me to pursue what dialectical behavioral therapy calls radical acceptance—completely and totally accepting with our mind, body, and spirit that we cannot change the present facts, even if we do not like them. Acceptance does not imply that we must approve of our circumstances. It simply means that we acknowledge them and understand that our disapproval won't change reality.

Radical acceptance is a proactive and ongoing process. I made the decision to practice it the day acceptance dawned on me at Mass, but I found myself having to reconfirm that choice almost daily as I was tempted to go back to resistance and escape my pain.

I remember being in crisis one day, battling anxiety, and feeling profoundly lost. I called my Emmaus sister who had also experienced loss and frequently gave me perspective and peace. I needed her wisdom. This particular day, she didn't seem as sweet and empathetic as usual. Instead, she said, "Betsy, I'm sorry you're going through this, but you have to understand that your daughter gave up her life to inspire hope and faith in many, and you are the one who needs to carry that legacy in her name." What I heard sounded more like, *accept it already because you have work to do!* It shook me to my core. I stepped out of my victim mentality and made the decision to stop fighting, to surrender. She helped me radically accept that moment.

Acceptance allows you to stop trying to change the unchangeable. It's about choosing to live in the present moment, rather than attempting to alter the past. With acceptance, you take a step back and allow yourself to feel, rather than resist. This moment is quite liberating, and it feels like the beginning of clarity and hope. You stop trying to control what you never had power over.

With acceptance came my need to believe in Heaven. If I was going to be at peace with my daughter's departure, I wanted to feel that she was in a "better place," as people loved to say (which annoyed me in the process). I "believed" in Heaven because it's what my parents taught me, but I couldn't imagine it being a better place than what Fofi experienced in our family.

I prayed for God to reveal to me that Heaven was real.

He answered clearly.

I was having one of those mornings of great resistance and sorrow. My one-year-old son was taking a nap, so I threw myself in bed to cry. I was sobbing inconsolably and praying for God to show me that Fofi was happy. If I had the certainty that she was, I could at least feel happy for her and act as the selfless mom I strived to be. I begged for an answer. I was hoping I could hear it from her in a dream so there would be no room for doubt or misunderstanding. That's why in rough moments I always went to my bed. I wanted to see her in my sleep and numb the pain in the process.

The doorbell rang.

I dried my tears and rushed towards the front door in hopes that it wouldn't wake up my son. I peeked through the door's peephole and saw a woman I didn't know standing on the porch. I opened the door, curiously.

The woman stepped into my entrance hall with a strong presence. With her chest up and powerful voice revealing confidence, she said firmly, "I've come here to tell you that your daughter is in Heaven and is ecstatic enjoying the presence of God."

Holy crap! I couldn't believe this was actually happening. I guess this is what people mean when they say that God spoke clearly to them. It is not that He personally comes and says in a strong and robust voice, "Betsyyyy, this is your answeeeer." Rather, He sends angels. In case you're wondering, the one who showed up at my house turned out to be our gardener's wife, whom I had never met.

This experience helped me accept that my daughter was in the real Heaven; not the one we created for her in our home. It also compelled me to radically accept that she was happy elsewhere. I had the choice of dwelling over missing her or being happy for her.

I imagined it was like having a daughter move to another country to live with the man of her dreams. On one hand, I would feel nostalgia because I would miss our day-to-day experiences. On the other hand, I'd be happy she found the love of her life and had the opportunity to thrive in a different environment.

I realize not everyone shares my beliefs. Someone who doesn't believe in Heaven may still struggle with accepting the death of a loved one. But here's the thing about beliefs: since they are not universal facts, we get to choose the ones that serve us.

The idea of finding hope in our daughter being in Heaven didn't soothe my husband's heart the way it caressed mine. However, the birth of Mia, contributed to him radically accepting the loss of our daughter.

For my client, Cindy, hope came from the belief that her 19-year-old daughter no longer had to suffer the cruel symptoms and treatments of her brain tumor. We have the power to decide what we believe to help our human minds let go of resistance.

To radically accept reality, is to adjust our expectation of what it should be into what it is. *My daughter had her whole life ahead of her. I was supposed to die before her.* This is what I thought was "normal" and was hoping for. But it's not what happened.

My reality is: Fofi left before me and her life cycle was complete in less than three years. That is what is. It is what I had to accept in order to start healing the pain of losing her physically.

My clients, Justin and Jessica, lost their 2-year-old daughter as they knew her. One ordinary day, they experienced the horror of finding her floating in their pool. Unlike Fofi, little Jasmine survived. She was victorious in a great battle against death. As a result of this ordeal, she suffered severe brain damage and ceased to walk, talk, and be her jolly self. Her parents were devastated. "She is not my daughter," Jessica said with a flat, numb affect that concealed the pain in her soul.

I looked her in the eye with compassion and said, "That is your daughter, Jessica, and until you accept that this happened, you won't be able to truly *see* her. Don't let her appearance distract you from embracing and loving the spirit you co-created with God in your very womb."

Tears escaped Jessica's eyes, revealing the pain she was restraining. I allowed for silence to create a space for her to connect with that emotion. I felt it deeply too. Jessica was struggling with acceptance. Hung up on the idea that this wasn't supposed to happen to her daughter, she escaped reality and the emotions that came with it. This created a disconnect with her Jasmine.

As homework, I asked her to spend time contemplating her daughter on a daily basis, particularly while she slept or showed no signs of disability. I suggested she observe her beauty, smell her scent, hear her breaths, caress her hair, and taste her cheeks with soft kisses. In doing so, she was to repeat to herself, "I fully accept and love you exactly the way you are."

A different woman came to my office a week later. Acceptance is a gift of hope and peace. In his book about mindfulness, Gregory Bottaro states that the path of acceptance is the one you walk with peace, but peace doesn't mean the alleviation of suffering. Peace is that deep interior stillness that tells you that no matter what kind of catastrophe might be happening in your life or in the world, everything is going to be okay. There is a sense of meaning to all of this, even if you can't understand it. It is the sense that someone bigger than you is in charge; that the weight of the world doesn't rest on your shoulders, and that it is ok to break down and not be strong enough."

Embracing pain as a fertilizer and engaging in radical acceptance are the key elements to a life free of suffering. In this life, pain only exists to nurture and teach you. Radical acceptance invites you to surrender fully to the *as is* nature of life and cease trying to bend reality. In doing so, you are freed from the suffering caused by resistance. You then have the power to invest all our energy on overcoming adversity and fulfilling your life purpose.

For an exercise that will help you proactively pursue acceptance, you may visit Hurt2Hope.com/FreeResources

CHAPTER 18

Interpretation

Life is, by nature, neutral. Shakespeare said it beautifully: *For there is nothing either good or bad but thinking makes it so.* We are the thinkers, the ones who interpret life, its events, and our experiences. We do so through our filter, our paradigms, and our ego.

Our filter is the lens with which we view the world. It helps us interpret information and stimuli based on what's aligned with our thoughts. Our thinking habits, in turn, are informed by the programing of our mind, which includes very ingrained belief systems called paradigms. Those powerful ideas we have on how to interpret the world come from our family of origin, societal traditions, culture, and life experiences. They have contributed to the formation of our ego—the identity we've assumed based on the habits and traits we've connected with throughout our lives.

Our filter, belief systems, and true self are not neutral. They are as subjective as their masters—us, human beings. Consequently, we don't see the world the way it is. We see the world the way we are because we experience reality based on our interpretation of it.

Life is neutral. We are the ones who interpret it in a positive or negative manner. Therefore, we have the power to determine how to feel about it by changing our interpretation. We own our worldview and, hence, the emotions that it exacerbates in us.

Five years after losing my daughter, my grandfather passed away. I adored him, but when he died, I felt a sense of peace amidst the pain of loss. He was 100 years old, suffered from dementia, and spent his last few days in a hospital bed with much discomfort. The same thing that caused excruciating pain years prior gave me relief because I would no longer have to witness my Grandpa suffering. Death, too, is neutral.

I remember one incident when I attended the Emmaus retreat. There was a nun who gave a talk and I felt compelled to speak to her. It was still too hard for me to use any derivative of the word death because I hadn't accepted that reality yet, so I told her I had a daughter in Heaven. As soon as she heard me say that, she smiled with deep joy and replied softly, "Oh how beautiful."

I wanted to punch her! I was so confused by her unempathetic reaction that I stood there as I tried to process her response. I couldn't, so I ignored it and kept on, "A week before she passed, we were in a pool and I told her not to be afraid because Mommy would take care of her… and Mommy didn't take care of her the day she was fearless. I couldn't bear the guilt of having failed her by not having taken care of her despite my promise."

Before the nun had a chance to respond, I had a revelation. A revelation is difficult for someone to understand unless they've experienced it. It is more than a mere thought; it is divine intervention. At that moment I saw our Blessed Mother, Mary, taking care of my daughter. I hadn't said, *"Don't be afraid. I will take care of you."* My words had been, *"Mommy will take care of you."*

Her heavenly Mommy was caring for her. In my vision, Mary held Fofi in her lap and embraced her. She sang my signature Little Butterfly lullaby to her, as I did nightly. The promise had been kept.

I felt the most incredible relief. I was so moved by my spiritual revelation that I walked away from the nun with a peaceful heart. I no longer cared how inappropriate I thought her reaction had been earlier.

As is everything in life, the nun's response was neutral, but I took it as an inconsiderate and unempathetic reaction. She must've truly believed in heaven the way I do now. I imagine she probably interpreted my statement, "I have a daughter in heaven," as a beautiful blessing, rather than the agonizing nightmare it was for me at that moment.

There was a disconnect between my interpretation of my daughter's death and that of the nun's. There was also much resistance and lack of acceptance on my part. And there was the expectation that people must be empathetic by connecting with others' pain, rather than dismissing our right to feel in our own way.

I realize we are human beings. The experience of pain is so real and powerful that it's hard to believe that what we feel is subjective, or simply our perspective. It seems impossible that what is so factual to us is merely an interpretation—a story we tell ourselves.

If I would've read this part of the book when my pain was raw, I would've thought: *How could this author suggest that this excruciating agony of losing my Fofi is self-inflicted? That it's a result of my interpretation of her death? Death is not neutral when we are talking about a young, healthy, and vibrant girl that happens to be someone's daughter!*

I didn't understand this then. I couldn't possibly. I had to go through my fertilizing pain and pursue acceptance to grow in wisdom. Only then was I able to grasp the idea that we have the power to create the way we see and feel about our circumstances. We are responsible for choosing the story we tell ourselves regarding life events and experiences we endure. Now I understand that, though I may not have control over everything I am exposed to, I do have the choice to view things in a way that serves me and frees me from suffering.

In his book, *I can't make this up,* Kevin Hart declared that life is a story full of chapters and that "the beauty of it is that not only do you get to choose how you interpret each chapter, but your interpretation writes the next chapter. It determines whether it's comedy or tragedy, fairytale or horror story, rags to riches or riches to rags."

Reframing

Understanding the importance of interpreting in a way that serves life best, I began practicing what became my favorite and most powerful clinical tool: reframing. When we reframe, we identify a thought or perspective that impacts us in a negative way, and we dispute it. We intentionally change it into a more positive version of it. We alter the standpoint with which we originally looked at the situation in question. We reinterpret it.

For example, I used to believe traffic was bad. The story I told myself was that it would make me late and it was an utter waste of time. It infuriated me when I got stuck in it! I felt frustrated and anxious. My reaction made sense because my interpretation of traffic was detrimental. However, the truth was that traffic jams didn't have the ability to justify my tardiness. Arriving late was nothing more than me failing to organize my schedule and calculate how long my drive might be. I could have left earlier, but I didn't. Traffic didn't make me late. I did.

I reframed traffic by reinterpreting it as a gift of time that allows me to be still and connected with the present moment. It also served as my inspiration to become more responsible with my scheduling, so that I may be considerate of others' time. Viewing traffic as a blessing makes me react to it in a pleasant manner. Every time I hit a congested highway now, I smile at the opportunity to be still and do things I often struggle to make time for. When I calculate my new estimated time of arrival and realize I won't be late, I also feel a sense of accomplishment because Miami traffic compelled me to create my brand-new habit of timeliness. Traffic is awesome!

Traffic is neither good nor bad. It is neutral. I used to see it as a waste of time. After practicing reframing, it became time well spent.

My dear friend Karla was diagnosed with breast cancer. A proponent of the vegan lifestyle, she spent years of her life nurturing and healing her body with all-natural remedies and plant-based foods. The thought of chemotherapy was overwhelming and went against her core beliefs regarding what we should feed our bodies.

Surrendering to her doctor's recommendation, Karla agreed to engage in treatment. I called her the first week of chemo to check up on her.

"How are you, my friend?," I asked.

I'll never forget her response. "I'm feeling great. They gave me the love potion and I imagined it healing my breasts, one cell at a time. The body is wise, Betsy. It knows exactly what to do. I feel so much peace."

"Wow," I said in awe.

I thought, *this woman is poisoning her body to kill both good and bad cells, and she calls the venom "love potion?"*

Karla knew how to reframe.

But wait, I got the traffic stuff down packed and chemo as a love potion was pretty impressive, but what is positive about losing your almost-three-year-old sweet daughter unexpectedly? Reframe THAT, Betsy!

Reframing is not easy. In fact, it may be one of the most difficult things we'll ever do because it goes against our natural reactions. As my dad would say, "We have to practice "violence" in order to reframe." In other words, we must attack our very own tendencies and habits to go against them.

Reframing can even feel wrong sometimes. *How could I reframe Fofi's death as a positive thing? Wouldn't that be morbid and evil? How could a mother be glad her daughter died?*

I am not glad Fofi died, even after having reframed her death. But I do acknowledge this devastating loss awakened me and has transformed my life in beautiful ways. At the beginning of my grief, the story I told myself was: *I am a grieving mother who couldn't keep her daughter alive and will never be happy again.* Every emotion I felt was in alignment with my interpretation. The way I carried myself suggested my misery. It was as if I had a sign on my forehead that read: "Mom of a 3-year-old that drowned." Ugh, it's still hard to write that word.

I hated feeling like people could tell. I often sensed their "pity" eyes on me and imagined them saying "That's her!" when I caught them looking at me and whispering back to the person next to them. I wanted to change this reality.

I couldn't bring Fofi back, but I could change the way I viewed her death. Doing so would also change the way people looked at me. If I was going to stand out, it was going to be because of the way I rose up from my loss, not by the loss itself.

I decided to reframe. Day after day I told myself that I got to be with Fofi all the time, rather than having to wait for her to get out of school. All I had to do was close my eyes, feel her presence, and spend some Mommy and Daughter time in a new spiritual way.

I also thought to myself, *I am a VIP in Heaven. When I ask her to intercede for me, she goes to Jesus and He's so crazy about her cuteness, that He can't help but say yes to whatever she asks for on my behalf. I then get all sorts of hookups in Heaven!* When I saw that these interpretations made me smile, even if for a second, I was inspired to continue changing my perspective.

After many years of reframing, I went from being the grieving mother that lost a daughter to becoming THE CHOSEN MOM OF AN ANGEL. *It takes someone special to mother an angel, so*

I must be among God's favorites, I told myself. *I am blessed to be Fofi's mommy and my love for her transcends death, time, and space.*

I reframe everything that threatens to rob me of peace. That's how I've become the boss of my life. In her book, *What I know for sure,* Oprah revealed that "The Creator has given you full responsibility for your life and with that responsibility comes an amazing privilege—the power to give yourself the love, intimacy, affection you may not have received as a child." This also gives you the power to interpret life in a way that allows you to thrive, serve, and be happy, while fulfilling your purpose in humanity.

Reframing is a process that requires faith, practice, and perseverance. It starts with discomfort, as is the case when we experience unpleasant emotions such as fear, sadness, and anxiety. Whenever you recognize these feelings, you must first sit with them.

Choosing to reframe before allowing yourself to feel may be a form of escape. Once you've connected with your uncomfortable emotions, you must pay attention to your thoughts. What is the story you're telling yourself about the situation you're in?

Here is the interpretation of a woman who wrote to me: "It is possible for SOME (not all) people to find joy, someday, a very, very, very long time after losing a child. ONE child. And after a long time where good things happened to them (e.g. more children, grandchildren, etc.). But for ME personally, it is not possible."

This lady had a triple loss when her son-in-law murdered her two grandchildren and her daughter. Her interpretation of such a tragedy is that it's impossible to heal from it: "I do not believe there is any recovery for this triple grief in this life, only the next life."

I understand her.

When we are in such pain, the darkness prevents us from even imagining that there may be light one day. Our mind confirms we will be miserable forever by focusing on the one thing that is aligned with our thoughts and feelings: SUFFERING.

Everything we see around us seems to inflict more pain, but it's really our interpretation that does that. It feels factual (and it is real), but it is only true for us viewing it in that light.

I once heard Chris Lee say that, "The moment we interpret, we become our interpretation." You see, it is not just that the way we view the world that affects our emotions. Our view also determines our fate. This is called a self-fulfilling prophecy in psychology.

A prophecy is when you say something is going to happen and it does. Self-fulfilling implies that you contributed to it becoming a reality. When you make an interpretation you also make a decision. This woman believes that she can never find joy again because her situation was worse than mine. I agree with her in that it was. I can't even imagine being in her shoes. My heart broke as I read her words.

But pain is pain, and that's what we overcome.

We don't heal the situations that inflicted the hurt. What we heal is the pain and emotions that resulted from those misfortunes. The darkness of that murder may seem impossible to overcome, but what she's feeling *can* be healed—as I have and you may—regardless of how different our circumstances are. However, if she continues to believe that she will "*...exist in the depths of hell until...*" [she dies and goes to heaven], she will fulfill that prophecy by giving up on this life and not pursuing proactively the healing and joy that is available to us ALL.

You don't need to know how you will ever be happy again. In the next chapter I will show you how you may be guided, so that you can access the step-by-step approach to your healing. All you need is hope that *maybe* you can overcome your tragedy too. Just a little faith will do. And, while you're at it, reframe!

For an exercise on reframing, visit
Hurt2Hope.com/FreeResources.

CHAPTER 19

Team

I've had many clients share that reframing is hard. It is, indeed. Not reframing, however, is much harder in the long term. It is detrimental to stay with your unquestioned paradigms and unchallenged assumptions that you are not resilient enough to rise from adversity.

You are. You have the strength and capacity to overcome anything, and the best part is you don't have to do it alone.

Choosing an All-Star team to support you will help you bounce back from painful experiences. It will help you grow and thrive. To surround yourself with people who are aligned with your values and desired outcome, is to set yourself up for success.

Create a team of friends, family members, mentors, and professionals who have the empathy and wisdom you need. Include people who inspire hope, lift you up, and are a step ahead in a similar journey. You don't have to know them personally.

I have mentors in my team who I have never met. I follow them on social media, read their books, listen to their podcasts, follow their advice, and even worship God as I sing along with them. They have no idea I exist, but they make me better.

Matthew Kelly, author and founder of Dynamic Catholic says that, "The people we surround ourselves with either raise or lower our standards. They either help us to become the best version of ourselves or encourage us to become lesser versions of ourselves...No man becomes great on his own. No woman becomes great on her own. The people around them help to make them great."

Who makes *you* great? Recruit people who support you without judgment and accept you just the way you are in the present moment. They must be willing to sit in the dark with you, but have the capacity to drag you into the light when hope is running low. They should hold you accountable when you become comfortable in your victimhood and fall into the temptation of suffering.

My two best friends, Zuly and Vale, were in my team. They gave me the space to feel. They hung out with me when I had nothing fun or positive to give back. They let me be sad and cried with me. I never felt pressured to "get over it."

Vale picked up some of my responsibilities when I didn't have the strength to perform them competently. She managed La Fofi's Rainbow Foundation when it was too painful for me to do so. Zuly listened and held me accountable. She took me to lunch one day and built the courage to tell me, "I understand you are hurting, but lately you are being apathetic and uncaring. You can grieve and still be kind."

She was right.

That moment changed me. I realized it was okay to feel sad, angry, and apathetic, but unacceptable to punish others for it. That is not the woman I was trying to become and Zuly reminded me before it was too late.

Different Roles

There is a right person for each need we have during adversity, and life in general. Some people will be amazing at listening, saying what you need to hear, and bringing hope. Others will do great with cooking, taking care of the kids, and making the day-to-day a little smoother.

My mother-in-law and Caruca were my angels in this department. Helping around the house and nurturing my kids, they gave me the time I needed to breathe and heal. I felt loved and supported through their acts of service. They never asked for anything in return.

My client's mother-in-law was also great with her children, but did feel a sense of entitlement for the help she provided. Mary needed her support after losing a child during labor. She was so depressed and devastated that she could barely get out of bed.

Arriving from the cemetery the day of the burial, Mary's mother-in-law followed her into the room, where my client threw herself on the bed, lifeless. Her mother-in-law told her she needed to get up and write thank you cards for everyone who attended the funeral.

Mary was outraged.

She felt it was insensitive of her mother-in-law to ask for such a thing. I agreed. But I knew her husband's mom meant well. She just wasn't equipped with the ability to sit with Mary's pain.

Realizing that her mother-in-law was not the ideal person to cry with, Mary created boundaries that allowed grandma to participate in her team by helping with the kids, but not taking part in the emotional support.

Not every player in a sport performs great in all positions. The same is true for the people in your team. Each person has a role they assume best.

Knowing this was helpful for my client, Linda, who was going through a divorce. Her Husband's betrayal, the loss of her marriage, and the ripping away of her children 50% of the time were just a few layers of her pain.

Her ability to create an all-star team assisted her healing. Linda called me every morning, when her anxiety was at its peak. She spoke to her Dad without saying a word and benefitted from his compassion. He always knew what she was feeling and when she needed a hug. Her Mom supported her through acts of service. Her Brother looked out for her and assumed the role of a handyman when things broke around the house. Her Sister gave her strength when her knees buckled.

Linda had a friend who didn't sleep well, so she reached out to her in the wee hours of the night to cry. She had Terry to take her out dancing and bring some fun to her somber days. Jackie was the best at bringing perspective. Laura took her out for bike rides and a breath of fresh air. Gabe invited her to lunch and gave her advice from a male perspective. Uncle Ted was on the bench of Linda's team, waiting to provide financial support when she needed it. God gave her peace.

Each person in Linda's team had a unique role, but they all shared a common responsibility: to do what they did best in a way that elevated her. They supported Linda in a manner that aligned with her desire to remain in integrity, especially when emotions threatened to derail her.

Hire & Fire

Like Linda, some people are fortunate to have a village they access to recruit their team. Others face the loneliness of grief alone.

Kelley lost her husband to an illness. He was her world, along with their two and five-year-old children. Kelley had immigrated from another country recently and had no community, friends, or support network. Her family was physically present, but emotionally unavailable. She needed help and hope.

Kelley hired me for both. Together, we found opportunities to build community and create a team that could support her through the grief journey. Opening up to moms of her daughter's peers evolved into beautiful friendships. She attended church groups that she connected with and participated in a retreat for widows, where she created long-lasting relationships. Kelley also engaged with social media pages that brought her hope.

It is never too late to create a village. Seeking guidance from a professional counselor or coach may be helpful, but sometimes you need something different. You determine that.

I was going to a psychologist before Fofi's accident. I didn't have much rapport with him, but it worked for what I needed from him at the time. I had hired him to help me overcome some unwanted patterns in my quest to become a better version of myself.

When Fofi died, however, I no longer felt safe with him. My husband suggested I schedule a session and even accompanied me to it. I couldn't even tell him what happened, so Alain did. The psychologist was unable to connect with my pain and seemed more uncomfortable than compassionate.

It was horrible.

I went home feeling emptier and more hopeless. I never called for another appointment, but what struck me was that he didn't reach out either. If any of my clients would've disappeared after revealing such a tragedy, I would've driven them crazy with follow ups, until I found something I could do to support him or her.

I fired my psychologist.

Having lost my professional counselor, I sought out a spiritual one. I reached out to Father Miguel, the priest with whom I engaged in the sacrament of confession during my Emmaus retreat. He had been such a light that day, that I always remembered him with gratitude.

Father Miguel agreed to see me and, for years, he took on the role of my spiritual and clinical counselor. Ever since, I've continued to have coaches and mentors who help me process, reframe, and grow from adversity.

In some instances, the professional you recruited for your team is an attorney, physician, teacher, or financial advisor. Having the right advice from them will greatly determine your outcome. Conversely, it will be detrimental to allow people, who are not aligned with your purpose, to influence you in a moment of vulnerability. They may lead you to decisions that feel right and relatable at the moment, but will cause destruction and regret later on.

Vicky was so angry at her soon-to-be ex-husband that she hired an attorney who would declare war and promised vengeance. She didn't think about how this would affect her mental health and the relationship she had with her teenage children. Following her attorney's advice, Vicky ended up with millions of dollars in debt, a strained relationship with her kids, and at the verge of a nervous breakdown.

She recruited her attorney based on her emotions, not her values.

Linda didn't make the same mistake. During her divorce, she sought out an attorney who protected her legally, emotionally, and spiritually. Her lawyer helped Linda see the pain in her husband when he seemed unreasonable. This helped her be compassionate, instead of vindictive. It enabled her to remain in integrity, and look out for the well-being of her family, while protecting herself.

Hire professionals who align with your morals, understand your goals, and who you trust have your best interest in mind. Fire those who won't lead you to hope.

Support Groups

At some point, I also tried a support group. Kathy, a woman I served through Fofi's Rainbow Foundation, invited me to speak at a group of bereaved parents she created. Moved by her initiative and humbled by her invitation, I eagerly accepted. Kathy had lost her 18-year-old son a few months prior, so I did my best to prepare a message of hope.

I invited Alain and my friend Natalie. I also met her through the foundation after she suddenly lost her daughter. Though she was in pain, Natalie radiated peace because she didn't allow the darkness of suffering to lead her. I instantly connected with her faith and hunger for hope.

We arrived at Kathy's house, where Alain and Natalie sat with the group while I did my presentation. At some point, I proposed a positive perspective of the pain we all had in common. With the corner of my eye, I noticed that Kathy, who was sitting next to me, started fidgeting and moving anxiously towards the front corner of her chair. I sensed tension, but didn't understand why, until I met with her resistance.

Upon hearing my hopeful interpretation, Kathy burst out saying loudly, "Well, I don't agree with that! It is not fair that we have to go through this..." She seemed angry, but all I could feel was compassion. I lovingly validated her feelings and explained my thoughts again in a way I knew she could connect with—meeting her where she was.

Kathy's grief was recent and raw, and I acknowledged that she wasn't ready to hear some of the lessons I was sharing. God knows I didn't care to hear about hope when all I felt like doing was throwing myself in bed and never waking up. That's why we must start our grief with acceptance of our pain and allow ourselves to sit with it. Only then, will we be ready to do all these things I suggest we work on here.

My response calmed Kathy down. She relaxed and moved back to occupy her entire seat. I continued for a little longer and concluded my presentation. After doing so, we all introduced ourselves and shared our stories. I was amazed to hear how my new friends lost their children—suicide, illness, accident, murder, and even choking with a piece of meat in a restaurant at age 20. My goodness! There was so much pain in those horror stories. I know from my experience that the cause of death can be haunting. The grief of losing a loved one is one thing, but the healing of how it happened is a totally different and parallel process.

I guess that's why so many of the parents in that meeting had taken so long to heal.

Pain is overwhelming when we try to address it all at the same time. Some of the parents had lost their child up to 10 years prior and still talked about it as if it just happened. It was heart-wrenching to witness their suffering after so many years. It was also scary to think that could be my destiny too. I wanted to honor my daughter through service, not tears. *But I'm not more special than these people*, I thought. *Am I being too optimistic or naive?*

As I doubted my goals, hope slipped away. Then my spirit shook me and reminded me of why I was there in the first place. I went to spread and get hope; not to be depleted of it.

I continued listening with compassion, until the last couple shared something that impacted me.

The wife said, "We are part of a club that we didn't choose to be a part of."

My heart rejected that statement. *Not me! I decide what clubs I'm going to be a member of! I respectfully decline one whose members are defined by the suffering of losing a child.*

My mind ranted: *I lost my daughter, but that doesn't define me. I am more than a mourning parent. There's more to my essence than what the title of griever could possibly encompass.*

I am a child of God.

It is not possible that He went through the trouble of creating me for some hopeless club. I will create my own club of risers—people who have lost, undergone adversity, experienced deep tragedies, and use them to grow and serve.

I couldn't wait to leave. Alain and Natalie shared my same feeling.

Attaching your identity to the title 'griever' is a choice. Grief, like pain, is fundamentally good. It is the journey towards healing. It is not, however, the final destination.

I once read a post on social media that made me cringe: *As grievers, we're never healed. We'll always have our grief. We can be "healing" and making progress towards happier days...but we'll never be healed, nor do I ever want to be. My grief is a part of me, and I'll carry it with me forever, just as I will with the love of the ones I've lost."*

I understand where comments like these come from because that's what it feels like when you're in the turmoil of pain. This perspective is founded in the idea that grieving equals loving. The more we loved the person we lost, the more we must mourn.

I reframed that socially imposed paradigm into *the more we loved, the more we push through to use our pain for growth and find the joy that will inspire healing in others. I honor my daughter through service, gratitude, and love.*

I'm not a griever; I am a beacon of hope because I have grieved.

I choose to surround myself with individuals who are aligned with my reframed interpretation of grief. That's why I never went back to the bereaved parents' club and decided to create my own support team. That is also why I join groups, participate in events, and read books that inspire hope and resilience.

I am not against support groups. In fact, I facilitate one as part of my Hurt2Hope online program, and it is powerful.

TEAM

I believe in support groups that come together because of a similar traumatic experience, but stay connected by a shared vision of hope. They define themselves, not by the trauma, but by the way they rise from it.

Who's in your team?

For a list of questions that will help recruit your team, go to Hurt2Hope.com/FreeResources.

CHAPTER 20

Habits

Some say we are like the people we surround ourselves with, but Aristotle insisted that "we are what we repeatedly do." Then Sean Covey updated this statement to "We <u>become</u> what we repeatedly do." This suggests that we are grievers if all we do is grieve, but we may become joyful and fulfilled human beings if we simply change what we do consistently. Engaging in healthy habits is one of the most defining factors of success in any area of our lives. Habits are especially helpful when we are enduring hardship and loss.

A habit is any behavior that is repeated regularly and requires little or no thought. Though habits may be so ingrained that they seem innate or even part of our personality, they are learned and are developed through reinforcement and repetition. Almost everything we experience in our lives is a habit; the way we think, the things we do, our reactions, our negativity or optimism, our faith, anxious feelings, fear, and even grief when we've engaged in it long enough.

A habit usually begins its formation in response to a real stimulus. If someone grows up surrounded by violence, they may develop the habit of fear, anger, or violence to defend themselves.

Children raised with nervous or pessimistic parents are more likely to grow up to be anxious and negative. Men who were told that *boys don't cry*, had to be strong, and "man up," may have a hard time being vulnerable and expressive in adult relationships. If you often heard or witnessed that what doesn't feel good must be avoided, you may be tempted to escape pain or responsibilities by engaging in self-destructive behaviors like procrastination and addictions. Even suffering, as a response to pain or loss, can become a habit.

All of these responses are sensible in the original circumstances in which they were formed because they served a purpose. Initially, they are reactions triggered by our minds to protect us from perceived harm. When they bring relief, they are reinforced by the positive results. Hence, we repeat them the next time and the following, until they become automated. This is how thinking, behavioral, and spiritual habits form.

Once ingrained, we no longer have to think about habits. They simply happen without us consciously instructing them to occur. They have been physically wired into our brains through repetitive performance. We know what shoe to put our foot in because we've done it our entire lives, but pay attention to how a one-year-old has to think about it and look for ways to figure out which one is the right or the left. Habits save us time and energy because they are stored in the basal ganglia, a different part of the brain from where our thoughts and decision-making processes take place (in the prefrontal cortex).

Research shows that adults make approximately 35,000 decisions a day (including which foot to put your shoe on). If we had to think and process each of those decisions, our prefrontal cortex would have so much activity that it would probably cause the brain to explode. That's why habits are important in keeping us safe and whole.

They are especially helpful when we are experiencing hardship because pain and worry tend to consume us. During trying times, our emotions deplete our willpower and thinking abilities. Having healthy habits frees up space in our prefrontal cortex, allowing us to use our limited energy to process our grief and make important decisions.

Habits are a gift that leads us to healing when they serve us in a healthy manner. The problem is when we continue to put into practice habits that formed to help us cope before, but are useless or detrimental now.

If you no longer live in a dangerous neighborhood, why respond with violence when you can simply set a boundary with words? If you are not being abused in the present moment, there's no need to be fearful and distrusting with people who love you. If all you could do back then to survive a tragedy was to numb the pain, keep in mind the situation is different and it may be safe (and healthy) to sit with your ache.

It is essential that we become mindful of the habits that will set us up for success to reinforce them during our healing journey. However, it is just as important to explore which ones are holding us back.

I used to always be on the go and commit to more activities than I had time for. I thought filling up my schedule and checking off boxes in my to do list was the equivalent of being productive. Boy was I wrong! Being so busy all the time was detrimental.

As I grieved the loss of my life as I knew it, I learned that my days were unpredictable. Pain showed up unannounced and demanded all my attention. Having a hectic lifestyle didn't allow me room to grieve.

I coped by either escaping my grief until it exploded unexpectedly or felt increasingly overwhelmed by the delays and accumulation of unchecked tasks. This way of processing further enhanced my already depressed mood and contributed to my feelings of inadequacy.

I thought having a "crazy life" was normal for the life season I was in. I had a husband, small children, a home, and a private practice that demanded my attention. I didn't think I had control over it. The truth is, I was so accustomed to living that way that I had grown to believe that always being on the go was my fate, rather than my choice. Grief taught me otherwise.

Stillness

One of the most important habits we must practice during adversity is stillness. This is when we quiet our minds and stop our bodies to simply remain with our true essence and connect with the present moment.

Stillness is the quality of being. Coming from a paradigm of doing, this was difficult for me to grasp. I was in so much pain that I wanted to do whatever it took to heal, or at least bring myself to becoming a functional human being capable of performing small tasks without breaking down.

I thought that's what healing was supposed to look like: having the ability to do, despite the pain.

Besides, stillness was *a waste of time* and way more painful than keeping busy. Doing nothing gave room to remembering the excruciating reality and grief I was in. As artist Marina Abramovic states, "The hardest thing is to do something which is close to nothing because it is demanding all of you."

Beingness is a safe place we can go to when we are experiencing hardship. Although it may feel uncomfortable and painful in the moment, it is a place of healing. As Ryan Holiday shares in his book *Stillness is Key*, "The world is like muddy water. To see through it, we have to let things settle. We can't be disturbed by initial appearances, and if we are patient and still, the truth will be revealed to us."

Sitting still with my muddy water and letting things settle made hope visible. It also provided guidance on my pathway to healing because beingness is wise like the depths of the ocean, unaffected by waves. In the end, during the time that I felt loss and most lost, the doer in me was fulfilled by doing nothing. Simply being when I really didn't know what to do was the best plan of action.

Stillness includes breathing, meditation, prayer, visualization, and mindful practices. It is also a walking in nature or a moment of connection and inner peace. Breathing, for example, helps change our brains neurochemically during times of crisis.

When we experience a painful life event or simply think of it, the amygdala in our brain perceives it as danger and releases oxygen to our extremities to prepare us for fight, flight, or freeze (our automatic safety responses). This means we are left with less oxygen in our brain's prefrontal cortex, where thinking and reasoning take place. That's why we feel shortness of breath and can't think straight. To recover that oxygen, breathing practices are most efficient because the amygdala is preverbal. That's also why we can't talk ourselves out of a crisis.

Before reasoning we must breathe oxygen back into the brain. Former monk, Jay Shetty, assures that when you learn to navigate and manage your breath, you can navigate any situation in life. Mindful breathing is a form of stillness where change begins. As Robin Sharma says, "Growth happens in the resting phase; not in the performing stages." Stillness precedes and enables wisdom.

For resources that will help you practice stillness, go to Hurt2Hope.com/FreeResources

Physical Wellness
While stillness is an important habit in overcoming adversity, it must be accompanied by mindful action. Many times, people confuse stillness with paralysis. Intentionally doing nothing is a spiritual practice, not a form of procrastination or laziness. When our grief is raw and recent, the most suitable action may be stillness and delegating.

I loved an analogy I read in *I wasn't ready to say Goodbye*. They said that when we've just experienced a loss, we must treat ourselves as if we were in an intensive care unit (ICU). We should let others take care of us, be still, and focus on recovering. However, when we've been discharged, it is time to proactively contribute to our healing and sustained health. We may be asked to nurture our bodies with whole foods and movement. At the beginning, it is possible that walking is all we can do. Then as we become stronger, we could find ourselves running a marathon! Our anatomy is linked to our psychology. Therefore, engaging in physical activity and healthy eating translates into more energy, better mood, and increased clarity of thought.

Exercise and healthy eating are keystone habits. This means that when we engage in them, the benefits bleed into other areas of our lives, providing healing and inspiration. It is okay to rest at the beginning of our grief journey, as if we were in ICU. However, after a few days or weeks of giving your heart the rest it needs to be discharged, you may be ready to take small steps in creating healthy habits.

Understanding that healing is not linear, there will be times in which you cannot get out of bed and it is healthy to give yourself the day off. But these days should be the exception. Your energy is consumed by your pain and your willpower is depleted, so you will never feel like working out. Do it anyway.

Starving ourselves because "we're not hungry" may feel right or binging processed foods may calm our anxiety and provide immediate relief, but they will hurt us in the long term. Nourish your physical gut and your intuitive gut will be fed in the process. This will enable digesting everything that comes our way so that we may discern and make decisions wisely.

After losing my Fofi, a high school friend from Puerto Rico formed a group to raise funds for the foundation by running a half marathon in my daughter's memory. A part of me was compelled to run with my friends, while the other side doubted that I could even make it a quarter of the way. I was also breastfeeding Mia at the time, who still didn't sleep through the night.

Waking up early to train would be a challenge, I thought. Then I remembered that there are two kinds of people: the ones that focus on what they want and those that focus on what *prevents* them from getting what they want.

I wanted to honor my daughter, and this was an opportunity to do so, regardless of the challenges. I didn't like running, but I loved showing appreciation to others' loving gestures, so I leveraged my value of gratitude to commit to the task. I'm also a woman of my word, so I knew that once I agreed to this, I would not fail my team.

Hours later, I started feeling anxious about the thought of training for a half marathon. *I can't run alone. I don't even like running! I won't know what I'm doing. What if I don't have what it takes? 13.1 miles is too much. I can barely run three! I can't wake up early. I have to pump in the mornings, so I'll be dehydrated before I even start training. What if I get injured?*

It's crazy how powerful our thoughts can be, but just because we think them, doesn't mean they're true.

In the end, our tendency to think negatively or from a place of fear, is also a habit or an automatic response from our brain, which thinks that anything different is dangerous.

I began practicing positive self-talk (another great habit) to ameliorate my anxiety, shift my mindset, and empower myself. *I can do this. My legs are strong, and my heart is healthy. Running is mental and my mind is powerful. I will run as if every mile was a step closer to embracing my daughter again. I will run to her and for her. I can find a partner that will train with me. I am able to take naps if I need to recover my sleep. I am energized. I am strong. I am capable. I am disciplined. I can do hard things. I GOT THIS!*

Just that "pump up session" was enough to lessen my anxiety and clear out enough space in my mind to focus on a plan of action. My friends were training in Puerto Rico and I lived in Miami. Having a running partner would help keep me accountable and motivated.

But who?

None of my friends ran. I reached out to the first person that came to mind: the woman that was "just there" the day after Fofi's passing; the one who stood alone under the thermostat waiting for me to need her. I needed her now! Caroline was not a runner, nor did she even work out at all. She was just a loyal friend I knew I could count on. I called her.

"Hey! I was wondering, is running a half marathon on your bucket list?" She hesitated, knowing this was a loaded question.

"Um, yea, maybe one day."

"Great! Because my friends in Puerto Rico asked me to run a half marathon for Fofi and I need someone to train with me. I thought you'd be the perfect person to do it. What do you think?"

Crickets.

"Hello?" I wondered if she'd hung up.

"Yes, Betsy. I'll train with you." No questions asked. No objections. No conditions.

Because exercise is a keystone habit, running with Caroline had a domino effect in both our lives. Being aware of how much work and effort it took me to burn calories made me more conscious when it was time to choose the foods I ate. I didn't want to cancel the effects of my workouts with a miserable cookie or bag of chips.

As a result, my body changed as did my self-image. I also became more confident in that I could do *all things*, as I was reminded by God's voice inside me the day my daughter died. Training for a half marathon also gave me one of the greatest gifts I've received: my Soul Sister.

When you work out, endure adversity, or embark on a journey with a partner, you share moments and stories with that person that unite you forever. You talk about things that you have no time to share about in your hectic life. You are inspired by thoughts and dreams that you never imagined possible. You break through walls, both physical and emotional, that make you feel invincible together. You support each other in unthinkable ways and grow in strength, wisdom, and grace.

In the end, how well we did the day of the race matters little compared to the unequivocal benefits of having created the habit of exercising and the bonds of friendship.

Caroline continued the habit of running (and became really good at it), while I focused on strength training after our race. I swore that I would never run long distances again. Running the half marathon was like childbirth. You don't regret it, but you don't necessarily want to go through it again.

Then Caroline's dad passed away. I felt her pain. I wanted to do something grandiose to show her how much I loved her. The first thing that came to mind was the one thing I didn't want to do, but she had done for me when I needed her. I agreed to run another half marathon in memory of her dad.

I couldn't wait to give her the news. But I wasn't expecting what she said next.

"I'm so excited! But I've decided to run the *full* marathon for my dad..."

Without hesitation, I replied: "No way, girl. How about I run the first thirteen with you and then wait for you at the finish line?"

Caroline laughed and told me she was grateful I was running the first half with her.

But as soon as I hung up, I got thinking. *Maybe I CAN run a marathon. I want to be there for her. I want to honor her dad the way she chooses. How amazing would it be if I could accompany her every step of the way and see her cross that finish line from behind. How could I say no to her? This is an opportunity to show her how much I love her. I must run this marathon. I can do hard things. Oh, crap. I can't believe I'm doing this!*

To seal my commitment, I bought a new pair of running shoes, snapped a picture, and texted it to Caroline with a caption that read: "I'm in."

In January of 2016, we completed the Miami Marathon in memory of Dr. Joachim De Posada. I ran all 26.2 miles without stopping or walking, and I enjoyed each minute of it. I was with Caroline every step of the way, as I had envisioned it. However, I didn't get to see her cross the finish line from behind. Though she was a better runner than me, that day my deep sense of purpose propelled me to move faster during our last stretch and, as I originally told her on our phone call, I waited for her at the finish line!

Moving your body doesn't just change your physique. It transforms your life. Working out when your body wants to lay on a bed and numb the pain with sleep is a habit that may save you from despair. It will energize and improve your mood with the release of endorphins. It may also help you channel your emotional stress in a healthy manner, while generating a sense of accomplishment. If you're lucky, you may also check off a race from your bucket list and find your soul sibling!

R & R

In our journey towards healing, finding a balance can be challenging. We are told to feel the pain, but not dwell on it. It is important to be still, but not to the point of paralysis. Similarly, exercising is a powerful keystone habit for our health, yet overexerting may lead to illness.

When our bodies are strained and exhausted, our brain has a hard time differentiating between fatigue and heartache. Because our energy is depleted, tiredness attracts low frequency emotions such as sadness. It is just too much effort to be excited and happy when our bodies are down. This is why replenishing our energy regularly is a necessary habit for our well-being. Fortunately, we have a free and effective way to do so!

Adaptation energy is the ability to handle our daily demands and unexpected events. Sleep helps restore our adaptation energy. Like willpower, it is consumed as we respond to challenges throughout the day. According to Don Miguel Ruiz, "Every day we awake with a certain amount of mental, emotional, and physical energy that we spend throughout the day."

We don't have the same adaptation energy in the morning after a good night sleep as we do at night following a long day of work, decision-making, traffic jams and emotional disappointments. Grief also depletes our ability to cope and adapt to our daily challenges. When we are in pain, we expend our will power with the constant effort required to manage our emotions, discern our choices, and function properly. A good night's sleep recharges us.

When we are in a depressed mood, we tend to be lethargic during the day. My client Tracy would take daily naps and then stay up late because she wasn't sleepy anymore. In addition to experiencing deep suffering when she was left alone, ruminating in the dark, she would find herself snoozing all morning. This caused her to be late and rushed or wake up drowsy. Before she was up, she had already expended lots of adaptation energy negotiating with the alarm clock.

Besides depleting your will power, the snooze button is detrimental for your health. A complete sleep cycle takes approximately 90 to 110 minutes, which means that our bodies start preparing to wake up over an hour prior to opening our eyes. The snooze only lasts nine minutes, so how restful can that sleep be? Tracy agreed to substitute the habit of napping by a 15-minute meditation session. This new habit helped her restore some energy for the second half of the day and still go to sleep at a reasonable time.

Before going to sleep, Tracy journaled or read to soothe herself with calming thoughts. In the mornings, snooze was no longer an option, with her phone alarm coming from the bathroom. She felt rested, even though she was waking up 20 minutes earlier. Tracy uses that time for her morning routine, which includes meditation and planning for her day. All these changes, which were preceded by the keystone habit of sleep, have transformed her life as she feels ready to conquer her day rather than find herself playing catch up.

Other clients have reported waking up in the middle of the night and not being able to fall back asleep. Learning how to soothe oneself with mindful practices may help solve this problem. It is important that we examine our sleep and reflect on how restful we feel during the day.

Struggles with concentration, memory, energy, and physical performance may suggest sleep deprivation. If that's the case, then planning and implementing a sleep routine that serves you will greatly contribute to your healing and growth. They don't call it beauty sleep for nothing!

Laughter

When my children were newborns, I could spend all day contemplating their precious little faces. Time stopped for me to gaze at their chubby cheeks, peaceful countenance, and spontaneous smirks. I especially loved it when they smiled, and I imagined their dreams. Their giggles were contagious. It made me grin until my cheeks hurt. At that moment, my joy exceeded the exhaustion from the sleep deprivation of those early days.

When we smile, the brain releases feel-good hormones that are associated with lowering anxiety and increasing feelings of happiness. We tend to think that we smile because we feel great, but research shows that the opposite is also true. As Nhat Hanh beautifully put it, "Sometimes your joy is the source of your smile, but sometimes your smile can be the source of your joy."

I like to think that smiles are God's antidepressants and have no negative side effects. They boost our immune system and relieve pain through the release of endorphins. Laughter really is the best medicine. Humor never failed to uplift Alain's mood either. It always transported him to a more optimistic and hopeful state, even through the most painful days. That's why he has friends that make him crack up in his all-star team. Some of them are comedians and show hosts he's never met!

When we endure hardship, surrounding ourselves with laughter makes us laugh too. Our brains are wired to automatically mirror a smile. Try making funny faces or laughing out loud hysterically at the dinner table and you'll see that—after thinking you've lost your mind—your family will join in. Laughter is truly contagious.

Practicing the habit of smiling and laughing will give you a respite from sadness and pain. You will not feel like seeking comedy, but humor contributes to your healing, so laugh anyway.

As I write the last chapters of this book, we are living through the world pandemic of COVID-19 and need laughter more than ever. With a new norm of wearing masks in public, compulsive hand washing, and bathing ourselves with antibacterial, I thought it would be appropriate to find some humor in this mess. Reader's Digest never fails, so here's a joke by Susan Freeman. I hope you enjoy it as much as I did.

"Since the outbreak, my 47-year-old son has been washing his hands religiously. In fact, he said, "I've been washing my hands so much that I found the answers to an old eight-grade math quiz."

To find your laughter again
go to Hurt2Hope.com/FreeResources

Positive Self-Talk

When we are going through difficult times, it is particularly easy to fall into the habit of negative self-talk. *I am such a loser. It is impossible to overcome this. I have nothing left to give. I'm horrible at this. I can't. Why work so hard sowing if the chance to reap can be taken away? I'll be alone forever. No one loves me. My life is over. I'll never be happy again.*

We would never speak to someone we love the way we often talk to ourselves. It is important to catch our negative statements and reframe them.

I had a professor in grad school who puzzled me with his response when I confided my struggles to him. "I'm so jealous I'm not in your shoes," he said. *How could this guy want to be in my miserable position?* He continued, "...because I won't be able to learn and grow from your experience. That's reserved for you"

This man reframed my interpretation about adversity. As I repeated this new perspective to myself (without believing it fully at first), I found myself feeling better and taking positive action.

Words matter. They penetrate our subconscious mind, which believes whatever we tell it. If we are constantly telling ourselves, verbally or with thoughts, that our life sucks, our subconscious will have no choice but to believe it.

It will then follow orders by creating emotions and behaviors aligned with that belief. Ultimately, this results in the self-fulfilling prophecy of misery. We don't end up exactly how we thought we would by chance. We drove ourselves there. Similarly, if we reframe those statements and reprogram our self-limiting beliefs through positive self-talk, we create our road to joy.

I love how Don Miguel Ruiz explains this in his book *The Four Agreements*. "Your word is the power that you have to create. Speak with integrity...Avoid using the word to speak against yourself... Use the power of your word in the direction of truth and love...Impeccability of the word gives you immunity from anyone putting a negative spell on you [including yourself]. You only receive a negative idea if your mind is fertile ground for that idea. When you become impeccable with your word, your mind becomes fertile for words of love." Hopeful self-talk leads to hope.

Tips to Creating Habits

In an effort to begin talking to yourself with the same love and compassion as you would to others, it is important that you follow the ASPR guidelines: Awareness, Substitution, Planning, and Repetition. These will help you mindfully engage in all habits that lead to joy.

Awareness

First, you must create awareness. If you don't know what your habits are—whether it's because you've attributed them to personality traits or simply haven't stopped to think about it—it may be helpful to do the following exercise.

Answer these questions sincerely and double check them with someone who knows you well.

When do you engage in practices associated with stillness, wellness, sleep, laughter, and self-talk?

What do your habits look like?

How do they affect your life?

What are your thoughts about them?

How could you improve these habits?

What prevents you from becoming better at them?

Are those obstacles entirely true, or is it your interpretation formed by self-limiting beliefs?

How can you reframe them to make the desirable changes happen?

What benefits could you acquire from engaging in superior habits?

Substitution

In our effort to engage in new habits, we need not start from scratch. Habits are best changed through substitution. The behavior we are trying to change is usually triggered by a stimulus.

For example, my client, Susie, experienced betrayal in her marriage and presented the habit of ruminating about the affair every time she was driving, showering, or waiting.

Rumination is the focused attention on the symptoms of one's distress and on its possible causes, rather than the solutions.

After exploring her tendency to pursue awareness, we realized that the stimulus triggering rumination was the act of being alone. Engaging in these disturbing thoughts yielded a reward: returning to her familiar role of victimhood. Though Susie consciously wanted to be proactive in forgiving her husband and finding joy, there was a sense of comfort and relief in being the victim. For that instant, she didn't have to focus on herself and could blame it all on her spouse.

Habits operate in a loop. First comes the stimulus, then the behavior, and finally the reward. In order to change a habit that doesn't serve us, as was the case of rumination for my client, we only need to substitute the behavior. The trigger and the reward should remain the same. Once aware of these two, we looked for healthy responses that Susie could practice in solitude.

Susie agreed to practice affirmations and positive self-talk. We made a list of reframed statements that described how she'd love to feel one day and recorded them. *I have a fulfilling marriage. My husband is loyal and honest. I trust him. I am loved. I am stronger than ever. I choose joy. I am in control of my thoughts. I think happy thoughts. I forgive easily. I live in the present moment. I am safe. I am respected. I have peace.*

Every time Susie was alone and caught herself having negative thoughts, she played the recording of her affirmations and recited them repeatedly. This new habit produced the same reward as rumination: relief. However, the solace she received empowered her, as opposed to enabling her victimization. Positive self-talk became a keystone habit that saved Susie's marriage, but also transformed her self-confidence and communication skills.

Planning

Once we've become aware of our habits and have determined the desired substitution, we must plan for it. Planning ahead is important if we want to succeed. Since habits are automatic and so ingrained, they happen effortlessly. The new behaviors, however, don't occur naturally. They're still occupying space in our prefrontal cortex, so they have to compete with everything else we have going on that depletes our adaptation energy. Our minds put the new things at the bottom of our priority list. Hence, no matter how determined we are to change, if we don't plan accordingly, it will be left for last or not happen at all.

After losing Fofi, I was erratic with exercising. I would do something here and there but was not being consistent. I finally made the decision to work out regularly, but it took me a whole year to actually accomplish it.

First, I sought to become aware of what was preventing me from committing to it. I discovered a whole lot of self-limiting beliefs! I learned that the best time for me to work out was early morning because of my schedule and responsibilities as a mom and wife. But there was a problem, according to my thinking habits.

I am not a morning person. I can't wake up at 5 a.m. because I won't be able to function with my clients. I can't go to sleep any earlier. I need rest more than I need exercise, and I don't have time for both. These were my limiting beliefs.

You would think that this whole habit changing thing would be a piece of cake for a therapist that takes pride in her ability to reframe and overcome hardship! But it wasn't easy. First, I had to change my self-limiting belief of not being a morning person.

Next, I reframed the idea of exercising in a way that would help me. Doing something because we "have to" does not provide the same reward that a habit with purpose does. I don't value physical appearance as much as being healthy, so I gave my own meaning to exercising and made the idea of committing to it irresistible.

Exercise will enable me to be an active mom that can carry her kids while hiking and jump in trampolines with them. It will help me release stress so that I may radiate peace to my clients. Working out will energize me and make me feel empowered.

Once I mastered these and my *"I love being an early riser"* affirmations, I still struggled to start. I understood everything rationally, but I'd still feel anxious the night before when it was time to set an alarm for 5 a.m.

As my final step, I decided to leverage another one of my strengths. I am a woman of my word and have great consideration for other people. If I hired a trainer, who was to wake up at 4am to be at my garage gym by 5:30 a.m., there was no way I would ditch him. I called him and scheduled our sessions. I set the alarm. The habit was sealed. No matter how tired I was or how many times my kids woke up at night, I never cancelled on him. My principles forced me to honor his time, but he also served as my accountability partner. I didn't want to fail him—or myself, really. I now crave my morning routine, as is the case with habits that have been ingrained in our lives.

Repetition

I didn't establish my exercise habit the first day of training, but it took that first, second, and third day to get there. Repetition is key in habits formation. It is also important to reap the benefits. I wasn't energized the first weeks, as I stated in my affirmations. I was exhausted. I still felt anxious every night the alarm was set up for 5 am, but I did it anyway. I persevered and now I'm blessed with a healthy practice that promotes my health, improves my mood, and allows me to be the active mom and wife that I dreamt of being.

Each day is an opportunity to deposit some effort into developing routines that increase your resilience and strength. In his *5 AM Club* book, Robin Sharma wisely shared that "your days are your life in miniature. As you live your hours, so you create your years. As you live your days, so you craft your life. What you do today is actually creating your future. The words you speak, the thoughts you think, the food you eat, and the actions you take are defining your destiny — shaping who you are becoming and what your life will stand for. Small choices lead to giant consequences over time. There's no such thing as an unimportant day."

Today is your day! What will you do to propel your journey towards your greatest self?

For ideas, go to Hurt2Hope.com/FreeResources.

CHAPTER 21

Spirituality Toolkit

F.A.I.T.H. (Fertilizing Pain, Acceptance, Interpretation, Team, and Habits) is the plan of action that helps reprogram your mind, so you can outsmart the habits, self-limiting beliefs, and perspectives that are holding you back. You can use all five tools to improve your lives, whether there's hardship or not. Instilling them as habits will inevitably transform you into a better version of yourself.

Viewing and embracing pain as a FERTILIZER helped me respond to unexpected and undesirable life events in a more graceful manner. I still feel the discomfort and sting of things not going my way, but I trust that they are training me for something bigger. Besides, I know I can do hard things. This attitude helps me pursue radical ACCEPTANCE.

When something out of my control is robbing me of my peace, I find myself reciting internally: *I fully accept this situation exactly the way it is.* Acceptance removes my resistance towards reality and empowers me with the ability to focus on what I can control. That's usually when I examine my INTERPRETATION and reframe it into one that helps me regain my peace.

Sometimes I have a hard time practicing acceptance and changing my perspective into a more positive one, so I reach out to someone in my TEAM. I have great friends and mentors who shine their wisdom when I feel stuck. Those days I'm particularly intentional about staying centered in my daily routine concerning healthy eating, exercising, and meditating. These HABITS equip me with an extra layer of protection that replenishes my adaptation energy and provides the strength I need to carry on.

F.A.I.T.H. is truly a powerful set of tools, but it is only effective if we practice it with *faith*. We must believe in the process, in our ability to do the impossible, and in a higher power that will help us through it.

Our human nature is glorious but limited. Our brains and bodies are extraordinary, yet finite. Our spirits, however, know no boundaries.

In this chapter, I will teach you how to reach your maximum potential and achieve the impossible by connecting with the divine within you. I call my higher power God, but please replace any reference of Him by what you name your Source. That's what I do when I read Eastern or New Age authors that share their wisdom from different perspectives. In the end, we are all ONE under God, the Universe, or Mother Nature.

ONE With God

As babies, we are born without the ability to distinguish between ourselves and the world. Our mom is our universe. We depend on her completely for food, growth, love, hygiene, and sleep. She is our "source."

Imagine life is a circle. As newborns, our circle fully overlaps with that of our mother's. We are one with her. Then, we grow and discover that we can move, eat, bathe, speak, and do many things on our own. We stop viewing ourselves as one with our procreator. Our circle moves away from that of our mom's, and they no longer overlap completely.

More time passes, and we grow into independent and self-sufficient adults. We rely on our own mental and physical abilities, needing less or no help from our source. Our circle of life connects minimally with our mother's. We become our own person with a fully developed ego, or sense of personal identity.

A similar process takes place between us and our heavenly Father. We are born to our spiritual life as babies who see themselves as one with God. We can't do anything without His guidance and assistance. Our spirit is pure and overlaps fully with His. But then our ego—the idea we have of ourselves—forms. We define our self-concept and learn to trust our own abilities, forgetting where they came from. We conclude that we can exist and survive without our Source.

Feeling empowered and invincible, we are seduced by cultural paradigms that brainwash us with the idea that strength and success come from our self-sufficiency. Just like we did with our mother, we drift away from God. We created a gap between our own spirit, which remains one with the Creator, and our ego.

It is appropriate, and healthy even, to become independent from our parents. In fact, they taught us how to eat, walk, speak, and act, so we may do it on our own. However, the mind is too limited to grasp the infinite wisdom of the divine. "For my thoughts are not your thoughts, neither are your ways my ways," declares the Lord. "As the heavens are higher than the Earth, so are my ways higher than your ways and my thoughts than your thoughts." (Isaiah 55:8-9)

We may survive with our human knowledge and capabilities. We can even fulfill astounding accomplishments and be content with our lives. But we will never rise up to the greatest self God created us to be, unless we reconnect with our true self—our spirit.

I've had many clients who call themselves atheists. I find it fascinating that they chose me, an unapologetic believer, as their therapist. However, our spirits unite us and I've had the most beautiful connection with every one of them. Even though they deny the existence of a higher power, I can see the divine in them and am drawn to their essence of love. We are all light by nature, regardless of our beliefs. We are all one under the Creator.

I've seen my clients who are non-believers apply the clinical tools they acquired in therapy to rise above adversity. They've shown admirable grit and determination. It is captivating to witness their improvement... until they hit *the wall*.

Human nature is finite. Therefore, our efforts eventually lead to a wall that reads "my maximum potential ends here." Too tall to climb with our bare feet, this boundary nudges us to request help in order to reach past the wall. Psychiatrist Carl Jung suggests we "put down roots like a tree, until clarity comes from deeper sources to see over that wall and grow."

The deeper source is our inner wisdom; the divine within us. It is that place in our spirit where we connect with God and become one with Him; where His superior ways and thoughts become our own. It is from that place that we can be elevated past our wall and soar like an eagle.

We can run far with our legs and discover greatness with our brains, but only with our divine spirit can the sky become the limit.

My client Mark came to me with a terrible and debilitating depression that kept him wanting to end his life. This young man considered himself an atheist. Mark was apathetic to people and chose to not engage with anyone at school. He worked hard in therapy to find some peace, but sometimes I felt I was working harder to keep him alive.

One day I felt particularly pleased and proud of how far he'd come along. He had joined school clubs and was no longer suicidal. Mark's energy had shifted and his smile had appeared. He was not where I knew he could be, but he felt content enough to exist in this life that was once unbearable.

Right after I met with Mark, another young man came into my office for the first time. Jack was a believer and seemed to be in a similar place in his life to that of Mark's. He was stable and had healthy social interactions but felt discontent. He believed there was more to his life than what he was experiencing, and knew he had a purpose he wasn't yet fulfilling.

At that moment, I realized that the equivalent of Mark's maximum potential was what brought Jack to therapy. Mark's destination was Jack's point of departure. It was not the end, but merely the beginning.

That's what happens when something or someone bigger than you has your back. You are limitless, powerful, and relentless. You feel in your core that there's more, even if you don't know what that looks like or how to attain it.

You're led by hope and inner wisdom, not by reason or what human eyes can see. You are guided by the 20/20 vision of the divine in you.

ONE With The Universe

Being one with our Source means breaking through the boundaries of our bodies and brains to access the divine spirit we truly are. However, oneness also suggests that our lives are purposeful and everything we think, feel, or do impacts the lives of others. We are part of a big family we call the Universe.

When I was grieving the loss of my Daughter, it was hard to show up for my loved ones the way I wanted to. I knew I had permission to feel the pain and it was justified to stay in bed all day, so I did at times. However, I chose to get up most days and hold my children with the same tenderness I embraced Fofi her last day of earthly life. I didn't feel like being intimate with my husband, but I showed up with a naked heart every night and whispered with my eyes, "I see you." I knew my grief would affect my family most, so I made sure to acknowledge them and get up every time I fell.

With time, I learned that they weren't the only ones watching. The world was paying attention too. People, including strangers, waited for me to rise so they could see it was possible for them too. As Mitch Almbom wrote in *The Five People You Meet in Heaven*: "each [life] affects the other and the other affects the next…and the world is full of stories, but the stories are all ONE."

If you feel that your pain is only hurting you, think again. This is not just *your* divorce, loss, illness, addiction, or failure. I have never been divorced, yet I've suffered its consequences more than once. Every time a couple I love (including my clients) separates, I go home with a broken heart. I have lost sleep, relationships, and peace over their rupture.

I've also hurt others with my stress, grief, and anger. "Hurt people hurt people," said Yehuda Berg, and I have two decades of clinical practice to prove it. If we don't assume responsibility for our own healing, we will offend and neglect the people we love most. Conversely, when we find wholeness in our Oneness with God, we no longer expect others to fill our voids. We become accountable for our pain.

I now look back at my darkest days and realize that my behavior threatened my family of losing yet another loved one, but this time to grief. There were days in which I was alive only because I was breathing, but I was adding nothing to the world around me. "The tragedy of life," according to Robin Sharma, "is not death, but what we let die inside of us while we live."

The deaths that hurt most are those of the people who are still alive.

Look around to see who you have neglected, abandoned, or offended while you engage in an affair with pain. Your life matters and your decision to remain in despair or find hope affects the universe.

You and I are ONE, and for you, I wrote these pages.

Prayer

Writing this book was a form of prayer for me. I needed so much strength that I found myself begging for the grace of God to help me carry on. It took me two years just to finish Part I. Each word I typed was a reminder of my daughter's death. I re-experienced the pain I felt in the early stages of my grief. I shed countless tears and found myself hyperventilating when describing—and reliving—my loss.

I prayed for peace.

Prayer is my favorite coping mechanism. It amplifies all clinical techniques by bringing hope. It reminds us that we are not alone and don't need to depend solely on our abilities.

Back then, my ego thought that prayer was the way we convinced God of granting us a request. *Please save her,* I begged Him the day of the accident. *I was raising her for you. Let me finish my job.* Who did I think I was? I mean, the guy is God! He must know what He's doing and whether or not my "job" was completed.

"Prayer is not a request for God's favors…Genuine prayer is based on recognizing the Origin of all that exists, and opening ourselves to it." This is how Cynthia Bourgeault beautifully explained the tool we use to communicate with our Source.

I understood the real purpose of prayer the day Mia was born. Waking up without feeling her all night in my womb, I sat in the bathroom praying for her to be safe. The déjavu of that *Please save her* prayer, generated a piercing anger in me. *Why pray if God is going to do whatever the heck He wants anyway?*

I called my mom for guidance. "Mom, Mia didn't move all night. I'm scared. I started praying and wanted to ask you to do the same, but then I realized that made no sense. God is God. He will do whatever He chooses regardless. Why waste my time asking for what *I* want?"

Lovingly, my mom replied, "Betsy, prayer is not for God. It is for you. It doesn't change His mind. It changes yours."

In an instant, I transported my mind to August 25, 2013—the day I prayed the most in my life.

My plea started with the *Please save her* prayer. *Make her heart beat!* I begged for a miracle. I reminded God of my faith and loyalty to Him. I was certain that He would listen and grant my request.

Seeing there was no progress, I wavered. I asked desperately for something I could repeat in prayer. Preparing me for what was coming, He answered, *I can do all things through Christ who strengthens me.*

No! Figuring this came from my own fears, I rejected the response. *God must grant my request because I am praying with immense faith.* I felt entitled.

Her heart still didn't beat.

Surrendering to His will, I fell on my knees and sang the chant of hope.

In a matter of hours, prayer changed *me*, as I went from demanding my will to accepting God's plan.

From there on, prayer kept me sane during a time in which the unbearable pain would have led me to insanity. It gave me something to do when there was nothing I could do. Prayer transformed my need to control what I had no power over into surrender. It humbled me and gave me access to my spirit, where divine strength lives.

Prayer deepened my relationship with God and brought me Hope. It was my way of conversing with the only one who truly knew what I was going through and had the power to make it all better.

Prayer didn't save my daughter the way I wanted her to be saved, but it rescued me from despair. It gave me peace when my mind was at war.

After speaking to my mother, I resumed prayer. I instantly found peace and, hours later, my rainbow baby was born.

New Beginning

Mia's birth reminded me of a story I heard at an event I attended. When a baby is in the mother's womb, she feels comfortable and content. The baby is enjoying the warm, cozy, and safe home she lives in. She can hear mom's reassuring heartbeat and is fed effortlessly through the umbilical cord. She has no desire to leave and is excited to continue enjoying her stay in mommy's tummy.

Nine months later, labor contractions threaten her peace until she's born to a world that's too bright and feels too cold and scary. For a newborn, birth is the death of her life as she knew it.

That same baby learns that she can continue to satisfy her hunger by latching on to her mommy's warm breast, where she can hear her heartbeat again. It's cozy in a different way, but a good way.

The newborn grows and can now walk as a toddler, read as a child, be cool as a teen, and become independent as an adult. The once terrified baby is loving this life and would—under no circumstances—want to go back to the mother's womb.

The same is true about this life we now know. We love it and are comfortable going about our days in a familiar and safe manner. But life is rarely stagnant. It's ever-changing nature threatens our harmony. Unexpected events, tragedies, diagnoses, separations, and failures can feel like death.

These experiences mark the end of our reality, but they also represent the beginning of a new life. In poet T. S. Elliot's words, "What we call the beginning is often the end and to make an end is to make a beginning. The end is where we start from."

The end of Fofi's life marked the beginning of Mia's because we would've otherwise become sterile. One doesn't substitute the other, but it reminds us it is possible to experience life after death and joy after pain.

Newborn Lesson
The end of my pregnancy introduced silence in my spiritual life. Once born, Mia's spirit called upon mine every night when she cried for breastmilk. There, in the silence of her room—interrupted only by the sound of her sucking on my breast—my newborn baby taught me about stillness. Time was infinite. There was no other place to be.

Despite my sleep deprivation, a comforting and pleasant feeling accompanied me in the night shifts.

I was fully present. I felt peace. I saw, smelled, and heard things I had never noticed before in my hectic lifestyle. I touched the softest skin and tasted the sweetest love. I took in those moments with all my senses and with the innocent curiosity of a baby.
Those nights, I didn't check off boxes on my endless to-do list, yet I felt efficient, connected, and alive. "Truly I tell you, unless you change and become like little children, you will never enter the kingdom of heaven" (Matthew 18-1-5).

My parents educated me on morals and doctrines, but it was Mia who taught me about deepening my relationship with the Divine through stillness.

Centering Prayer

Mia watered a seed that my aunts planted years prior. Titi Neyda, the one who invited me to embrace the pain, and Titi Tere, my mom's sister, practiced centering prayer. They worried about my lifestyle and suggested that I start this form of silent prayer to slow down.

Titi Neyda and Titi Tere complained that I was always running around like a chicken without a head. They said this would help train my mind to rest and become more efficient through stillness. I wanted to try it, but *I had no time* and I figured I was *too hyper to be able to quiet my mind anyway*. In my ignorance, I didn't understand that was actually the point. I was the ideal candidate for this spiritual practice.

Centering prayer, like traditional meditation, helps high achievers find rest in their minds as they clear out space to make room for creative thinking. It also aids people who feel overwhelmed by emotional pain.

Entering into a state of silence, solitude and stillness quiets the outside noise and allows us to tap into our inner wisdom. It simply reveals our spirit—the greatness hiding behind our busy brains. Quietude also reveals the answers that no amount of reasoning can disclose. Time invested in silent prayer is returned by the efficiency, clarity, and peace we acquire through the practice.

After years of resisting and making excuses, I finally decided to incorporate the practice of centering prayer into my spiritual life. The keystone habit of waking up early to exercise helped. It gave me the time and drive to devote to silence. I was enjoying the strengthening of my physical wellness, so I felt inspired to do the same for my spiritual growth. The domino effect of healthy habits continued to allow for transformation in my life.

Centering prayer is a method of Christian meditation developed by Catholic monk, Father Thomas Keating. Like many forms of stillness, the practice is most efficient when we practice it twice a day for 20 minutes. However, it may be helpful for beginners to start with 5 minutes at a time and increase it gradually.

Centering prayer consists of sitting in silence and gently introducing and repeating a sacred word, such as love, peace, or Jesus. It can also be a phrase like "Come, Holy Spirit," "Be still," or "Jesus, I trust in you." This sacred mantra symbolizes our consent to the presence and action of God within us. It's like telling the Holy Spirit, "Hey, I'm all yours. I surrender my ego to you and welcome your infinite love, peace, and wisdom inside of me."

Through this form of prayer, you place your ego in the backseat and are driven by the divine in your spirit. You do so by remaining still and quiet. You don't worship, praise, thank or ask God for anything. You simply remain in silence and solitude.

When your mind wanders—because it will—return to your sacred word. Every time you daydream or engage with a thought, you let it go by repeating your mantra.

I thought the idea of silence was to master meditation by emptying my mind of thoughts, which I didn't think I was capable of. However, this practice welcomes our distractions as an integral part of our lives. It simply encourages us to disregard them, as if they were background noise. We learn to acknowledge the thought but choose not to engage with it.

The fruits of centering prayer are reflected in our active life. We don't practice it to improve our meditation skills, but to enhance our lives.

After years of practicing stillness through this method, there are times in which I go on a brief journey toward bliss and peace. Other days, I spend all 20 minutes repeating my sacred word over and over again because of how distracted I am. Either way, my life is being centered by the presence of God within me.

This ritual turned out to be the tool through which I, and hundreds of my clients, conquer all challenges. Although I engage in silent prayer every morning, I also turn to it whenever I feel depleted, overwhelmed, or need discernment in decision-making. It allows me to top into my inner wisdom and open up my possibilities.

Silence turned my attention from my wailing heart to a peace "which surpasses all understanding" (Philippians 4:7). It also guided me towards healing.

If you are ready for such peace, find valuable resources at Hurt2Hope.com/FreeResources

CHAPTER 22

GPS

We often know what we want but have no clarity on how to get it. At this point, you've already learned great tools that will help you go from adversity to prosperity. In my online program, *Hurt2Hope*, my clients often struggle with not knowing exactly how and when to apply these skills. They wonder where the fine line between embracing pain and dwelling on it is, or how to identify the distinction between escaping and mindfully letting go. What should acceptance look like in their particular situation and how can they reframe their interpretation?

In *Hurt2Hope*, I hold my clients by the hand through this journey, but I ultimately teach them how to find divine guidance so they don't always have to depend on me. Similar to the mother-child analogy, my role as a coach is to help them soar on their own, whereas superior divine guidance may always remain within them.

Using God as your Global Positioning System (GPS) is the ideal way to know how to arrive at your desired destination. It gives you clarity of where to turn and what tools to apply every step of the way.

When I need to go somewhere I've never been to before, or want to see what the fastest route is to a familiar destination, I turn on my GPS. Positioning systems, such as Waze and Google Maps, get information from satellites that have a bird's-eye view of the route. This allows the app to determine the best way to arrive at the end point, considering obstacles out of my sight, such as traffic, accidents, and dead ends.

God also has a greater view of our life map. He can see our past, present, and future. He knows our hearts, struggles, and strengths. All this knowledge allows Him to guide us through the route that will elevate us to our highest self and help us arrive at our purpose. Consenting to our Creator as the GPS of our lives provides us with *guidance* (G), the ability to live in the *present* (P) moment, and the benefits of *surrendering* (S) to Him what is out of our control.

Guidance

One day, I turned on the GPS to go to Coconut Grove, a lovely neighborhood in Miami, FL. I planned on driving down the same route I ran through during my marathon training but needed directions for the exact location. I was going east on Sunset Drive when Waze prompted me to take the exit to Highway 826. I thought, *Ugh, this dumb GPS. If I continue on Sunset, it'll be faster and a more scenic drive.*

As the knowledgeable woman I think I am, I went straight and disregarded the app. I was approaching the upcoming traffic light when I heard the annoying lady on the app, "Recalculating. Make a U-turn." I rolled my eyes and ignored her. I continued going straight, and she insisted, "Recalculating…recalculating…recalculating!" *OMG, this thing is so annoying. I don't want to go through the highway. This way is better!*

I turned off the volume of my useless GPS. As I neared the Cocoplum Circle, one of my favorite parts of this beautiful route, I spotted the red lights of a Fire Rescue truck and a traffic jam that brought my car to a halt.

I felt enraged and frustrated. *I'm never gonna make it on time now. What do I do?* I looked down at my phone.

Recalculating.

My GPS had tried to warn me all along, but in my arrogance of knowing better and wanting my way, I failed to obey. Like Waze, the Man Upstairs is always available to direct us, but only if we turn Him "ON" and listen. He's a gentleman who won't intrude in our journey, unless we consent to His guidance.

My clients and audiences often ask, "How, Betsy? How do I turn God on as my GPS and hear his directions?" My simple answer is, "Meditation." For me it was Centering Prayer, but for others it may take the form of breath work, mindfulness, sound, chanting, yoga, body movement, or any other form of spiritual connection that aligns with their beliefs. Stillness filters the outside noise, allowing you to listen to the voice of God within. It clears out space in your mind to download divine wisdom.

I imagine our Source going around like Santa Claus delivering guidance. He throws bags of peace and clarity down the chimney of our spiritual homes, except in the ones that are clogged with human debris (e.g. negative thoughts, self-limiting beliefs, fears, arrogance). When He passes by those houses, he realizes there's no space available for what He has to offer. Saddened, He continues holding on to that wisdom until that person is ready to clean up the obstruction and open his heart for divine guidance.

Ignorance and arrogance kept me from receiving God's directions. First, I didn't understand the powerful action behind stillness. I also didn't think I could attain it with the hectic lifestyle I had unconsciously chosen.

Then, I assumed the *I know better* attitude that kept me trusting my intellect above my spirit. I thought my PhD, traditional prayer, and an hour a week at church equipped me with the knowledge I needed to guide myself toward joy. Just like I disregarded the GPS on my way to Coconut Grove, I judged silence as inferior and unnecessary. Gosh, was I wrong!

I can't think of someone better than my 40-year-old client, Erica, to illustrate the power of living a guided life. She is a single mom of four who had to come up with a million dollars within six months to avoid prison time. In addition to assisting her in her mindset reprogramming, I accompanied Erica on a spiritual journey.

She attended therapy weekly, but I asked that she also visit the Blessed Sacrament daily. She practiced silent meditation there, while consenting to the presence of the Holy Spirit within her. She found peace and comfort through this form of prayer. As the deadline approached, Erica became anxious because she didn't even have a stable job.

Throughout our process, she encountered many situations that required her to discern and make a decision. Do I sell my house, or do I prioritize a secure shelter for my children? Should I sell my properties, or do I wait for them to go up in value? Do I retaliate or keep my integrity? Every time one of those questions arose, I helped her be still and wait for guidance. Reluctantly, she did.

One day, I felt guided myself as I advised her to hold off on some decisions. I reassured her that the money would come, but she had to be patient and trusting of God's plans for her freedom. I didn't know how she could make a million dollars in the three months left, but my spirit was convinced that she would. I listened and obeyed by relaying the message.

I won't deny that I freaked out when I finished the session and realized what I had told her so confidently. *Betsy, you're crazy*, I thought to myself. I may have even called my husband right after to say, "*Baby, is there a way we can borrow a million dollars by this date if something doesn't work out?"* For a second, I became fearful that my intervention may have come from me, rather than the divine, but I just knew in my heart that things would work out.

And. They. Did. Step by step, God presented Erica with people, opportunities, and ideas that earned her one million dollars in two months.

Albert Einstein said, "We cannot solve our problems with the same level of thinking that created them." The affliction I endured after Fofi's death came from my human interpretation of that tragedy. Similarly, Erica got herself into the legal problem with a greed mindset. Elevating our level of thinking to divine wisdom awarded me the joy I have attained after my loss and my client the freedom she so desired.

In addition to helping us overcome hardship, divine guidance enables us to make wise decisions for our uncertain future. I have two clients who made important life choices at the end of 2019. Chris decided not to move out after his wife had an affair, even though she was not showing the regret and grace he expected. It didn't make sense to him and people judged him harshly, but Chris was operating from his spirit; not the reason. Something within told him to be still and not make the decision yet.

Another client, Sally, left her job after 20 years to accept a position at a prestigious corporation that paid double her salary. A go-getter intellectual, Sally was sure this was the opportunity of her life.

In March 2020, the global pandemic of COVID-19 hit Florida. This unpredictable crisis turned unreasonable decisions into wise ones and vice versa. The quarantine forced Chris and his wife to spend more time together, contributing to experiences that led to forgiveness and reunification.

On the other hand, the quarantine led to a tank in the economy, which resulted in Sally being furloughed. Though highly qualified, she remained unemployed for long months because most corporations were in a hiring freeze.

Chris and Sally had no way of anticipating a global pandemic, but our Source knew it was coming. Having turned to God as his GPS enabled Chris to continue working on his marriage when it made no sense to his own mind and mental health. He was guided by the Holy Spirit. As a result, he created a fulfilling relationship with his wife, which made his dream of keeping his family together a reality.

Notice that what made Chris' decision ideal is not the outcome of saving his marriage, but the process that led him there.

Sally was driven by reason, until her loss taught her about divine guidance. After experiencing severe anxiety, she devoted her free time to connecting with her Source through meditation practices. The woman who defined herself by her intellect and career became centered. This enabled her to create a thriving business, where she combined the newly gained spiritual skills to her corporate expertise. "Now I'm really unstoppable!," she exclaimed joyfully in our last session.

Guidance from above may seem unreasonable to the human mind. Therefore, we must use peace as the internal gauge that helps us discern. If you experience anxiety or lose sleep over a decision, do not go for it regardless of how much sense it makes. If you feel peace, despite how painful that choice may be, think no more.

When you follow directions from *"God's* Positioning System," you eventually reap the benefits of your obedience. It may not happen overnight and you will doubt, but be still and faithful.

When you have a hard time discerning, set your conflict as an intention for your spiritual practice and wait patiently for wisdom. God may not reveal your answer, which will come with a deep sense of peace, until the very second you truly need it. Do not waver. God is never a second late. His timing is perfect.

Life In The Present Moment

God shows us the way to our dream destination step by step, just like driving apps. Rather than giving us a printed map with all the directions at once, He enables us to trust and remain in His presence by revealing just our next move.

It's like driving in the Georgia mountains late at night, when it's pitch dark. Your headlights only let you see about 350 feet ahead, but you rely on them confidently. That's how we are called to be with our Father; trusting in His plan. He will illuminate our spirit with wisdom as we need it and will *recalculate* our path when we drift away.

This moment by moment process teaches us how to live in the present. Chinese philosopher Lao Tzu suggests that when we live in the past, we become depressed; when we live in the future, we develop anxiety; but when we live in the Now, we experience peace. What a powerful truth! I have witnessed this with my clients and can attest to it personally.

The darkest, most excruciating part of losing Fofi was the way it happened. I kept revisiting the scene by the pool and ruminating about what I could've done differently. My flashbacks pained me as if they were still happening. The accident wasn't what created my hurt. That moment had vanished. It was gone. Only I could inflict my own heartache by bringing to my present moment the emotional responses that belonged to the past.

The same was true for my client Tania, whose husband had a lengthy affair. Despite the fact that he did everything in his power to prove his sincere repentance and assumed responsibility for it, she kept dwelling on the details. It was hard to let go of them.

Tania, as is humanly expected in such a situation, was living in the past. Her husband was no longer disrespecting or offending her, and she knew this to be true, but she continued to feel the pain of the offense. There was nothing for him to fix because he had already done so. All he could do was sit with her in the dark and validate her feelings.

He did.

Tania's husband agreed to the unimaginable to regain her trust and prove his remorse. He stayed up every night to answer all her questions. She had access to every communication device of his. He took her to work with him and stopped providing services at the place the lover worked. He attended therapy, even when he didn't believe in it. Tania's husband proved his commitment to her and now it was her turn to do the work.

Tania realized that she was reacting to her own judgments about the affair; not the offense per se. The infidelity was no longer present. Demonstrating remorse and accountability, her husband was engaging in trustworthy behaviors. He had never been more loyal in their 25-year marriage.

Tania agreed to engage in daily meditation. Her husband joined her. Within weeks, her ruminating thoughts gradually dissolved into thin air. Her spiritual practice reduced her anxiety and freed her from her suffering.

This beautiful couple has been happier than ever before for over two years. They still send me pictures regularly to share in the joy that came from such a deep spiritual connection.

Tania proved that what happened yesterday cannot affect us today, unless we let it. It is our own lingering thoughts about a situation in the past, and the emotions they exacerbate, that rob us of our peace. As Robin Sharma said, "the past is a place to be learned from, not a home to be lived in." The spiritual practice of stillness enables us to heal that past and leave it where it belongs.

The word present is a synonym of gift because that's exactly what the NOW is for us humans; a gift. It gives us the opportunity to leave what hurt behind and reframe our current perspectives in a way that lifts us.

Fofi's accident happened, but she is not drowning right this moment. In my reframed visualizations, she is currently skipping joyfully around heaven, surrounded by colorful flowers. Why worry about the pain of yesterday, when I imagine joy shining in her smile today?

Eckhart Tolle says the present moment is all we have and invites us to make it the primary focus of our lives. "Time isn't precious at all," he continues, "because it is an illusion." Time is just a concept that we humans created to fit in our minds something too grand (or too simple) to grasp.

It's our way of making sense by treating as finite what is infinite. Now is the only time there really is. The past was "NOW" when it took place and the future will be the "NOW" if we make it there.

I love the wisdom imparted in the anonymous poem read in many 12-Step Programs around the world: *Yesterday, Today, and Tomorrow*. This piece of writing expresses that there are two days in every week that one should not worry about: Yesterday and Tomorrow. It reveals that Yesterday has passed forever beyond our control. It is gone, along with its mistakes, faults, and pains. Tomorrow, on the other hand, is beyond our immediate control, along with its possible adversities, burdens, and larger promise. Today is the only day left and it is then that "any man can fight the battles." The poem ends as follows:

It is not the experience of TODAY that drives men mad.

It is remorse or bitterness for something which happened YESTERDAY.

And the dread of what TOMORROW may bring.

Let us, therefore, live but ONE day at a time.

This reminds me of my client Tony, who was an excessive and aggressive drinker on the verge of losing his marriage. He attended Alcoholic Anonymous and had an interesting conversation with his sponsor.

"I don't think I can live without ever drinking again. One day I'll go to Italy and won't be able to have a glass of wine with my wife... and how am I supposed to go to Scotland and not have some whiskey with my boys?"

"Tony, you're not in Italy or Scotland right now. You can worry about that when the time comes," his sponsor replied wisely.

Five years later, Tony went to Tuscany with his wife and enjoyed the most beautiful scenery and delectable cuisine with a gratifying glass of sparkling water. What he thought would be excruciating was no longer a concern for him.

One. Day. At. A. Time.

Whether you're struggling with an addiction or going through loss, hardship, health or relationship issues, living one-present-moment-at-a-time is key to carry on with hope and grace.

Surrender

During times of adversity, it may seem you've done everything in your power to move forward, but nothing works. You feel depleted and with little left to give. When this happens, you must try the one thing that never fails in freeing you from suffering: Surrender.

Surrender takes place when you decide to radically accept the situation you're in and willfully give up your attempts to control it.

The need to control comes from the ego; not from our true self. It is a manifestation of fear, arrogance, insecurity, or weakness.

Surrender, however, results from exercising our power to allow for divine guidance to take over. It is having the wisdom to turn on the GPS and be still. It is what we do when we remove the resistance holding us back and proactively work on accepting our reality.

Surrender brings you hope and leads to calm. In Eckhart Tolle's words, "Anything you accept fully...will take you to peace. This is the miracle of surrender."

As humans, we have an idea of how life should be. These are paradigms that are ingrained in us as truths.

Parents die before their children.

If I am a good person and do no harm to others, I will be rewarded with good fortune.

Hard work yields success.

Life is fair.

I won't get sick or gain weight if I have healthy habits.

Tragedies only happen to bad people.

Moms should be caring and dads protective.

Young people have a whole life ahead.

Marriage is forever.

Good partners don't get cheated on.

Friends are loyal.

Innocent people don't go to prison.

We were all created equal.

We get what we deserve.

My kids will succeed if I'm a devoted parent.

Our children should marry someone we like for them.

That won't happen to me.

I have control over everything in my life.

Whenever something doesn't fit into the model of what we believe is right, we resist.

That can't be!

She was too young.

What have I done to deserve this?

It's not fair!

Our paradigms guide our reactions toward what goes on in our lives. We judge what people say or do based on our beliefs, and we interpret life events accordingly. These perceptions—the stories we tell ourselves—become our truths.

They say the truth hurts, but I believe it is *our* truth that hurts. Our interpretations are what create our feelings; not reality itself. If we view something as positive, we feel happy, excited, and peaceful. When we see an experience as negative, we exacerbate feelings of sadness, anger, and frustration.

Welcoming reality without judgement helps us manage our emotions. Doing so is challenging and often requires we surrender the limiting beliefs that are causing our suffering. Only then, will we be able to accept what is as is.

Surrender, unlike what most people think, is a sign of strength. It is not to be confused with giving up or accepting defeat. Quite contrary, surrendering is an act of courage. "The greatness of a man's power is the measure of his surrender," said William Booth.

It is hard to question what has been ingrained in our minds our entire lives. It is even more difficult to become aware that what we believe is true, may just be a perspective. Most people can't acknowledge that their unpleasant emotions are self-imposed. It takes someone brave to dig deep within and assume responsibility for one's heartache.

From a spiritual standpoint, surrender means intentionally submitting to the will of God for us, instead of insisting on getting our way. Rick Warren says, "You cannot fulfill God's purposes for your life while focusing on your own plans." Surrender requires that we be flexible with our path, but it does not deprive us from choosing our ultimate goals.

Turning to God, as illustrated in the GPS analogy, gives you the opportunity to clearly state your desired destination. In fact, He wants to listen and grant your greatest dreams. If they are what's best for you, He was the one who planted them in your heart anyway. The problem is, we often confuse destination with route.

In my earlier example, I wanted to get to Coconut Grove, but was attached to going through Sunset Drive. I failed to surrender to the GPS because I insisted on getting my will on the *how*. I was operating from the ego and that know-it-all attitude that often gets me in trouble. Had I followed the directions from Waze, I would've made it to my final destination.

Surrender is the method by which we welcome divine guidance and obey its directions, even when it seems to be taking us through the road less traveled.

My client, Olivia, was going through a separation. Her husband moved out of the house because he felt unhappy in the relationship. Olivia's main source of pain seemed to come from her resistance and inability to accept that this truly happened.

She kept ruminating about why he left and what she could do to get him to go back. She spent much time talking about and evaluating his behaviors. Focusing on the one thing she had power over (herself) was not her priority.

In one of our sessions, I shared with Olivia that she seemed more worried about avoiding divorce and what people would say, than rebuilding herself to attract her husband back. She was attached to the route (staying married to maintain appearances) and lost sight of the end goal: finding peace and joy again.

Olivia engaged in daily rituals that included the habits of exercise and mindful meditation. This centered her and provided relief for her anxiety. She finally surrendered the process to divine guidance and redirected her efforts to work on her spiritual growth.

She ceased to resist reality and stopped trying to control her husband. Soon, she found hope amidst her pain and her husband became intrigued by her newly acquired peaceful aura.

Olivia's relationship with her husband improved, but they remained separated. She didn't save her marriage. She saved herself, by finding peace through acceptance.

Surrender *is* the path to our final destination—be it healing, joy, success, peace, health, or strength. The journey may not look how we envisioned it, but it will always be better.

I begged for God to save my daughter because I ultimately wanted her to be safe and happy. He didn't rescue her from death, but I know in my heart that she is risen and has never felt more alive. My ways are not God's ways and, for as long as I have the wisdom and awareness to do so, I will choose surrendering to Him.

If you want to join me, you will need three things: hope, trust, and courage.

Hope is believing that, even when things are not going well, they will get better. I love how John Lennon said, "Everything will be okay in the end. If it's not okay, it's not the end."

Trust is the virtue that allows us to know confidently that the person we are surrendering to has (1) the wisdom to guide us and (2) our best interest in mind. Only if we trust the source to whom we will surrender our path, will we be able to build the courage to let go.

It is scary to relinquish control, but necessary to do so when we are ready to accept reality and end suffering.

According to Debbie Ford, the author of *Spiritual Divorce*, "surrender is the ultimate sign of strength and the foundation for a spiritual life. [It] affirms that we are no longer willing to live in pain. It expresses a deep desire to transcend our struggles and…commands a life beyond our egos." Our ego wants power and control; our spirit seeks inner peace.

My client Jane is having a hard time discerning what comes from her ego and what emanates from her spirit. She is going through a divorce and is in the middle of an excruciating custody battle. Jane, 35 years old, feels that her small children are not safe at Dad's because he's had problems with substance abuse and other erratic behaviors. She also has deep heartache and resentment towards him. Jane told me in tears that she was trying to do the right thing, but felt the world was conspiring against her. No matter how many mistakes he made, the judge kept giving Dad chances to stay clean in order to give him the 50/50 custody.

She was afflicted, fearful, and anxious. I reminded her that the unease and distress she felt are usually what *Recalculating* looks like when we live a guided life.

God speaks through peace.

He may not deprive us of the fertilizing pain necessary for growth, but he will always grant us the gift of inner harmony, if we are surrendering to His will.

Attempting to shed some light, I said, "The bumpy road, or "conspiracy of the world," is a sign that you're going the wrong way, Jane. If your ultimate goal is that your children be safe, happy, and cared for at Dad's, why does it matter if it's 20 or 50 percent of the time? It is your ego that wants to control the *how* and possibly punish dad. Stick to the final destination (the safety of the little ones), but surrender the route. Your husband is far from perfect, but he loves your children and has always been kind to them. It just may be that they need their dad more than you think is reasonable. Or maybe it is you that requires more alone time to nurture a future relationship, and God is already creating the space for you."

I heard a sigh. "It's just so hard."

"It is."

Our ego wants power and control. The spirit seeks inner wisdom through peace.

For me, surrender meant having faith that pain would elevate me, while God held my hand throughout the journey. Surrendering in the early stages of my grief sounded something like, *God, you're crazy! I don't know what you were thinking when you allowed her to die... but I will trust you.*

Testing the power of surrender helps us mature in the way we practice it. After many years of submitting to God's will, I respond differently when there's an unpleasant or painful situation. I recently felt devastated when I saw a year's worth of efforts go down the drain. I had been working really hard to build something in my business, and it was falling apart.

After having my pity party, I went for a walk. I was enjoying nature when I smelled poop. I looked around to see where the stench came from and noticed a fresh layer of fertilizer at the base of a tree.

I laughed at the reminder and looked up at the sky. *Okay God. I see you're fertilizing me. I'm actually getting excited about the mega surprise you have for me. It must be amazing because this thing that I'm going through really sucks!*

A sweet 15-year-old girl modeled this mindset when she shared her favorite scripture before a major surgery that would impair her ability to walk for months: "For I consider that the sufferings of this present time are not worth comparing with the glory that is to be revealed to us" (Romans 8:18).

What a precious and wise soul this Bella is! She understood that, since pain is a fertilizer, we need not fear it or escape from it. Instead, we may allow ourselves to feel it with grace and gratitude, knowing that our glory is in formation.

Bella's message was heaven sent. Recognizing her as an angel from above was also part of my surrender. It is unlikely that God Himself will show up at the screen of our GPS and scream at us *Turn left, Make a U-turn, Recalculating!!!*

In lieu of such a grand appearance, He sends people who have also surrendered to His will and are devoted to serving with guided wisdom. These come in the form of doctors, nurses, teachers, therapists, lawyers, mentors, friends, family, first responders, strangers, or any human being open to saying or doing what God puts in their heart. Our job is to trust them, so that our Lord's perfect plan for us may be fulfilled through their intercession.

When we learn to surrender, we acquire the gift of living a guided life. Our headlights are always shining on, sheltering us from the darkness of suffering.

Pain becomes growth.

Failure turns into lessons.

Illness creates strength.

Loss yields gain.

The end marks a beginning.

Surrender makes us whole. It shreds our entitlement and expectation to have our needs met by others. It teaches us how to look within and fill our own voids with divine grace.

Giving the wheel of our lives to God, we learn to see and love ourselves the way He does. We find a sense of peace that is immune to the disruption of external sources. We reconnect with our spirit and become One with the divine.

In other words, we "return to love." In her book with this title, Marianne Williamson explained that, "We were born to make manifest the glory of God that is within us. It's not just in some of us; it's in everyone. And as we let our own light shine, we unconsciously give other people permission to do the same. As we are liberated from our own fear, our presence automatically liberates others."

Healing ourselves with divine guidance makes us—and the world—better.

To learn practical tools that will help you surrender, visit
Hurt2Hope.com/FreeResources

CHAPTER 23

Purpose

Our lives have meaning, and so does the pain we experience. When I attended confession at the Emmaus Retreat, I had a life-changing conversation with Father Miguel. I confessed my self-centeredness as one of my sins. I was self-absorbed by my pain and failed to even acknowledge the need in others. I also told him about the darkness and flashbacks that haunted me.

Father Miguel shared a personal story of loss to validate my feelings with compassion and then shone divine wisdom. "Betsy, something that helped me with my dark images was to acknowledge them and then shift my focus to something else…"

I knew what he meant with this because, though it's hard at the moment, our conscious mind grants us all the ability to change what we pay attention to. He continued, "When you shift your focus, do so to an act of service. You may also work on becoming more selfless and mindful of the people around you."

Father Miguel's advice may have been simple, but it impacted me in a profound way. It felt like a therapy session. I left with renewed hope and was excited to take action.

From then on, when the flashbacks popped into my mind, I shifted my focus to acts of service. One time, I called a loved one who was struggling with her son's disability. When I couldn't act immediately, I prayed for whoever was losing a child at that moment.

Ambulances triggered me, so whenever I heard sirens blaring, I shifted my focus to praying for the ones being transported. *Lord, please keep that person safe and give peace to the family.* Now it's just become a habit to send love to people I witness in accidents, the news, or strangers on the streets. This practice, which came from my deepest pain, has made me a better person.

Healing Through Service

The thing about heartache is that it creates such discomfort, that you are willing to do whatever it takes to get rid of it—even become a better version of yourself. Just a small shift in focus can transform your hurt into hope.

I often tell my clients that life is like a bright white wall. It's pure, smooth, and peaceful. When you encounter adversity, failure, loss, or hardship, a small black dot appears in the middle of the white surface. You can't stand the disruption of the stain on your wall and obsess over it. It grabs your undivided attention and prevents you from looking at all the white blessings around.

Hope surrounds all painful experiences like a silver lining. You just have to shift your sight a bit. I can't think of a better way to do this than through service.

Service repels suffering.

Sorrow is too selfish to share space with generosity.

When I was actively serving families through La Fofi's Rainbow Foundation, I wrote personalized letters to include in the care packages we sent. These were heartfelt notes in which I connected with their pain and conveyed my empathy. I hated staying up late to write them and transporting back to deep affliction. I cried a sea of tears, but in time, that very salt water healed my deepest wounds.

Helping others is a powerful way to mend your broken heart.

Finding Purpose

We have the opportunity to serve on a daily basis by finding purpose in everything we do with the people around us, or even in solitude. You can define purpose by reframing or changing the way you view an activity.

When I'm home alone cooking or cleaning, I am really creating a pleasant space and meal for my family. If I write a blog or record a video, I am creating content to uplift my community. When I cook my famous Puerto Rican dish or do laundry for someone going through hardship, I am working as Jesus' helper. When I pray for someone, I am sending love and strength their way.

Even while I do things for myself, I'm serving. When I exercise, I am elevating my family life by being able to jump on trampolines with my children and go on outdoor adventures with my husband. If I read a book or attend a seminar, I am learning to better serve my clients. Everything I do is inspired by a deeper sense of purpose.

My career as a psychotherapist and speaker is no different. People often ask how I can do what I do. "Doesn't it rehash the pain? How do you deal with so much misfortune?" My profession is hard. Specializing in grief, my job is to sit in the dark with my clients and be the bearer of hope and guidance for them. This was overwhelming for me too.

I was very comfortable in my career being "the couples' whisperer," as my clients and colleagues called me. I was sure God created me to help save marriages and teach people how to thrive in their relationships. Maybe this was His purpose for me at the time.

Something happened after Fofi's death. Widows, grieving parents, bereaved siblings, and even divorcées came to me after losing their loved ones. Witnessing the raw suffering of their loss was hard, but I still had the couples to bring some humor to my days. Their experiences were painful too, but they shared funny stories that broke the somber tone of pain. When they talked about flying underwear across the room, while folding clothes during an argument, we couldn't help but burst into laughter.

One day I met with my marketing director, a very intuitive and faithful man. Aware of the new trends in my private practice, Jonathan wondered out loud if I wanted to mindfully shift the focus of my speaking and clinical careers to pain and adversity.

"NOOOOO! I'm the couples' person. I can't be 'the grief lady.' People will not connect with my perception of pain and they won't relate to me. I don't define myself by loss. I am more than a mom who lost her daughter. I just can't do grief. No way!"

Unfazed by my defensive reaction, Jonathan insisted with grace, "But what if that's what they need; someone who knows pain and can help them see it in a different light?"

"Absolutely not. I'm the couples' person."

I left his office feeling distressed. My heart pounded with unease. I was usually very receptive to his counsel because I trust his wisdom and knowledge. But I just couldn't accept this.

He's wrong, I tried to convince myself.

I got in my car and, as I exited the parking lot, I sobbed. *I don't want to be the grief person, God. Pleeeease! Don't make me do that.*

Recalculating...

I *am* that person now. Over time, I received too many nudges to ignore. I stopped resisting and found peace. I also felt God fill my heart with enthusiasm about the idea of helping others turn their hurt into hope. I finally surrendered.

That's the thing about surrender. When our heavenly Father plants a seed in our spirit, He also waters it with joy.

His will becomes our dreams.

I didn't want to be "the grief person," but I am delighted to be a beacon of hope for others. This new focus in my career has allowed me to fulfill my utmost desire, which Dr. Julie de Azevedo's song describes beautifully: "I want to be a window to His love, so when you look at me you will see Him; I want to be so pure and clear, that you won't even know I'm here, 'cause His love will shine brightly through me."

My life purpose is to be the face of God for the people I serve. When you reframe your career like that, you can't possibly feel like it's only about rehashing the pain.

So when people ask how I can do this for a living, my answer is, "How could I not?" I am the person my clients choose to share their raw pain with. I am the one they trust and feel safe with. I accept this grand privilege with humility and gratitude.

Nietzsche said that "He who has any *why* to live for can bear almost any *how*." My why is clear. I want my pain to mean something. I refuse to waste it, so I use it to bring hope to the hopeless.

Our why often becomes clear through pain. Sorrow has a way of revealing the meaning for our existence. In his book *A Man's*

Search for Meaning, Holocaust survivor Viktor Frankl wrote, "The way in which a man accepts his fate and all the suffering it entails, the way in which he takes up his cross, gives him ample opportunity—even under the most difficult circumstances—to add a deeper meaning to his life. It may remain brave, dignified and unselfish. Or in the bitter fight for self-preservation, he may forget his human dignity and become no more than an animal. Here lies the chance for a man either to make use of, or forgo, the opportunities of attaining the moral values that a difficult situation may afford him. And this decides whether he is worthy of his sufferings or not."

Dr. Frankl suggests that pain is such a gift, that we must deserve it. Pain is not a punishment; it is the fountain of wisdom, grace, and incorruptible joy. It takes seeing through the misfortune to capture the lessons within and only those who choose not to waste it are worthy of the growth it awards you.

You are a piece of a grand puzzle we call the Universe and you are responsible for leaving this world better than you found it. If you let it, your pain will build character and help you create impact, so you may fulfill your role in this planet.

My purpose is to keep my daughter's memory alive by spreading hope. Fofi's life was short, but complete. She affected the few people she could reach in her limited time and with her little size.

However, her purpose transcended death and is now being transferred onto you, through me.

Her legacy lives on and, hopefully along hers, mine will too.

Love Legacy

I have a memory of Fofi holding her newborn brother that caresses my heart every time I think about it. The same day of my C-section, I was at the hospital bed breastfeeding when she asked to carry Gabriel, who still hadn't earned the nickname *Gordi* (meaning chubby).

She sat on the blue visitor chair and got ready to hold him by putting her sweet hands together—side by side—as we do when trying to retain as much water as possible. She hadn't turned two yet, so the space created by her cute little hands was miniature.

It was adorable to witness the innocence and love with which the new big sister awaited to fit her baby brother in her tiny palms. She looked down at the cradle she created with her hands and back up at Alain, signaling confidently that she was ready to hold Gordi.

"Me, me, me…" she insisted when Alain approached the chair with my son in his arms. Daddy brought him closer to Fofi and accommodated him on a pillow between her hands and her lap. Fofi giggled nervously. She kissed her brother and caressed his face in awe. The joy in her countenance was contagious. The thought of it still moves me to tears.

I have a video of that moment that I watch over and over again. In it, I asked her, "Fofi, are you going to take care of your little brother?" "Yes," she responded firmly. She did, but only had one year to do so by his side. Every day at bedtime, Gordi recites the "Guardian Angel Fofi" prayer we created and blows a kiss to her looking at the ceiling. He never goes to sleep without saying, "I love you, Fofi."

Gabriel only knew his sister for 12 months, but the effect her life had on him remains eternal. He keeps her memory alive by continuing her legacy of love. Gordi treats his little sister with the same tenderness Fofi treated him. Mia is now emulating that deep affection with her baby cousins. There is a piece of Fofi's love in each of their interactions. I guess it's true what playwright Robert Woodruff-Anderson said, "Death ends a life, but it doesn't end a relationship."

Fofi will forever be my daughter. She taught me that true love needs not be earned by the beloved. Fofi no longer does anything to inspire my love, yet I continue to be enamored of her. She doesn't hug or kiss me—and she sure didn't fulfill my dreams for her life—but I love her with the same intensity with which she once welcomed her baby brother into the world.

Love is a legacy that often leaves us vulnerable. As the Spanish Proverb says, "Where there is love, there is pain." But the opposite is also true. Where there is pain, there is an opportunity to find love.

Love is the light that ends darkness; the hope that makes the sun rise; the hand that lifts us up. It is the ultimate measure of success for a life well lived.

If we live long enough, we will all suffer the consequences of poor decisions, life events, betrayal, failure, tragedies, or adversity. These experiences give us the opportunity to dwell in darkness or rise to love. No matter how obscure and impossible to overcome the situation seems, Love can heal it.

Love, and you will rise above pain.

Love, and you will find purpose.

Love, and you will arrive at Hope.

CHAPTER 24

Hope

When we face adversity, joy seems too far to reach and our emotional state can't relate to such possibility. Hope, however, is the lifeline that keeps us afloat in the middle of hardship. It gives us reason to push through because we believe that someday—somehow—things will get better.

Everything a living organism does is because of hope. We eat because we hope food will satisfy our hunger and nourish our body. We get in the car because we expect it to turn on and drive us.

Where there is hope, there is life.

Eric is a testament to this. He came to my office with a friend after almost jumping off a balcony the night before. In his early 50's, Eric had gone through every adversity imaginable. He experienced death and war while he was in the military. He lived through physical and emotional imprisonment during his years in jail, where resentment consumed him.

Eric had tasted heartbreak, loss, and psychological imbalance. In our first session, he confessed that he had wanted to commit suicide every single day during the last 20 years of his life.

"Why didn't you?" I asked cautiously.

His response was one of the most beautiful lessons anyone has ever taught me.

"Because I always think I may be really close to happiness. I wonder, *What if tomorrow is the day? What if my joy is right around the corner?* This keeps me going because I don't want to miss it if it's that close."

Hope saved Eric's life. For over 7,300 days, it kept him from pulling the trigger. It's been years since our time working together, and Eric has finally made it "around the corner."

It turns out that the reason he felt he was so close is that his inner wisdom was nudging him to pay attention. Like Eric, we often let outside forces rob us of our joy or look for solutions in the exterior. Meanwhile, the real antidote to our suffering lies within.

Hope buys us time to connect with our spirit and tap into the divine wisdom that will show us the way to a joyful, purposeful, and fulfilling life.

Hope propels us forward if we take action. Instead of wondering if joy was around the corner, Eric took the necessary steps to create his desired victory. He changed the passive nature of his self-talk to one of determination: *What if tomorrow is the day... that I accomplish the dreams I've been working for today?*

Hope must exacerbate, not excuse.

When you hope, you proactively pursue the outcome you seek. If I expect the train to take me to work, I drive myself to the station; I don't just sit around at home wishing the train transported me. Similarly, if I hope to rise above my heartache, and become a better version of myself in the process, my initiatives must direct me there. Hope inspires action to convert hurt into healing, growth, and joy.

I am free from suffering, even though I continue to experience pain and hardship. I don't know if I am fully healed or if such a term is appropriate to describe the ever-changing human nature. I thought I had overcome my loss when I started writing this book two years ago, but I learned there was so much more to heal.

Revisiting my memories to share the details with you took me back to the raw pain of the early days. Tears, flashbacks, and heartache seduced me, but I disarmed them with my welcoming attitude. *Come on in, my dear Pain. Do your thing and help me heal. Thank you for your lessons and the virtues you bestow upon me to elevate my life.*

In her Book, *What I know for sure*, Oprah shared that Maya Angelou taught her to express gratitude in the face of adversity: "Say 'Thank You' because your faith is so strong that you don't doubt that whatever the problem, you'll get through it. You're saying thank-you because you know that even in the eye of the storm, God has put a rainbow in the clouds."

To this beautiful description of hope, I add, "Say 'Thank You' because pain is fertilizing you. It is helping you grow to flourish as the best version of yourself that will help you become "a rainbow in someone else's cloud." Maya Angelou taught me that.

Our pain is another's healing. I pray that my loss may be your rainbow.

It doesn't matter when or if you fully heal. It's even pointless to worry about how long it will take before you stop feeling the pain. You get to embrace it as the path to joy. One day you will rejoice, and it is then that you'll realize you arrived at your final destination. At that point, you may still have moments of sadness, but they won't consume you.

Your glory will have superseded the story.

If you are hurting, know that this discomfort is temporary, but its resulting byproduct will earn you a lifetime of joy.

My name is Betsy Guerra, and I am the happiest woman on earth *because* I have endured loss. For that, I am grateful.

Five Minutes

I'd like to end our journey with a story that gives me hope and I pray it does the same for you. I feel and communicate with my daughter daily, but sometimes her spiritual presence is not good enough for my human self. On those days, I practice visualization.

I close my eyes and transport myself to Heaven, where I hope to be someday. I imagine I'm there with Fofi, surrounded by flowers of bright colors, beyond the ones I've ever witnessed. The grass is perfectly trimmed and is so soft that it feels like a rug caressing our bare feet.

The scene is pleasantly embellished by the fragrance of gardenias and the touch of her hands on mine. Her big round eyes are lit with love and her smile radiates a blissful glow. The soft wind caresses our faces and causes Fofi's curls to bounce, almost to the rhythm of the angelic songs in the background.

Our gazes interlock. We don't have to say anything to tell each other everything. We smile and embrace in a hug so tight that I can't tell where she ends and I begin. We are connected by pure love—one that surpasses all understanding.

I feel exhilarated when I realize I never have to let go. I think back to my time on Earth and it seems so insignificant that I can barely recall what it was like to be without her. *Oh my gosh, what was I so upset about? That was just five minutes! I get to be with her forever and ever now. What are five minutes compared to eternity?*

I think of clients whose kids have gone away to college. At the beginning they missed them dearly and suffered the detachment. Four years felt like forever, but then graduation came in what seemed like *five minutes*.

Their children returned and got married. They became grandparents and lived happily ever after. Those clients never dwelled about the college days after that. *Who cares about those five minutes of discomfort when they have the rest of their lives to enjoy their kids and grandchildren?*

My Fofi went to "college" a little earlier than I expected, but it will still feel like five minutes one day. The same is true for you. No matter what loss you've endured—the loss of a loved one, your marriage, a relationship, your health, freedom, self-love, expectations, dreams, or your life as you knew it—it will just hurt for five minutes.

This too shall pass, my dear friend. Just make sure you don't waste your pain in the meantime.

Make these *Five Minutes* count.

You are now ready to transform your hurt into hope!

Acknowledgments

Writing this book is the hardest thing I've ever done. It brought me to my knees when I relived the raw pain of the early days. For that, I'm grateful. The experience of pain has healed and transformed me into a better human. I wouldn't have been able to process it that way if it wasn't for my mentors' guidance.

My number one Life Coach is truly the one responsible for this book. Thank you, My dear Lord. Thank you for trusting me with such a beautiful project and giving me the strength and determination to push through. Thank you for inspiring my mind with wisdom and moving my hands as I typed every word of this book. Yours is the glory. I pray that you inspire hope in my readers and grant them your peace.

My mentors—Susan, Silva, Luly, The Giners, and Caroline—thank you. Susan, I am forever grateful for your love and guidance. The way you sat with me in the dark and had the courage to accompany me through it, moves me. You challenged my limiting beliefs and helped me heal.

Thank you for editing my work at the crack of dawn and helping me create this story gracefully. Thank you for the yummy lunches with fresh greens from your garden. I love and appreciate you so much.

Silva, it is because of you that this book was born. I was writing another one on relationships and communication, when you said, "You must start with your story." After meeting with my resistance, you insisted without wavering. I obeyed. I never went back to the other story. Thank you for being God's messenger that day and for your continued love and support. I am truly grateful for everything you do to help me spread my message of hope. Thank you for believing in me and my purpose. I love you, my friend.

Lourdes Antonia, how I love you! You were my first coach ever and the one who taught me much of what I know now. Sometimes you did it as the authority and other times you led me through your vulnerability. Either way, you inspired me to use my pain to serve. I admire you profoundly because you, too, have used your ache to uplift others. Thank you for being my role model, my teacher, and even my student. I can never thank you enough for your love and support.

Jonathan and Erica Giner, I am profoundly grateful for you two. You lead and serve with your heart, and that made all the difference for me as your student. Thank you for

ACKNOWLEDGMENTS

teaching me about life, business, and faith, when all I hired you for was marketing. Thank you for holding my hand and guiding me patiently to help me reach the unimaginable. Erica, special thanks to you for making time to help me with the graphics designs and book cover. I trust you and admire your talent. I love you, Giners.

My dear Caro, you are my mentor, my friend, my Soul Sister. This book is as much yours as it is mine. Thank you. Leading by example, you have inspired me to write, speak, and "sharpen the saw." How did I get so lucky to have you in my life? You love, serve, and give with all your might, and I am grateful for that. You have been there in the good times, but you have especially been present in the painful moments. Thank you for your unconditional support. Thank you for the countless hours you spent teaching me how to become a better writer, while editing this book. Thank you for our walks and therapy sessions...for listening and imparting wisdom. I don't know what I would do without you. I love you, Sis.

Besides my mentors, I am deeply grateful for my book-reading angels: Zuly Chaves, Vale Corrales, Cristina Pérez, Laura Bonich, Dr. Kuhn, Daisy Blanchard, Natalie Pizarro, Sasha Luque, Suzanne Sacasas, Jess O'Brien, Cristina Sánchez, Luly B., Caro de Posada, and Carolina Martinez. Thank you for believing in me and loving me enough to stay up late on weekdays and support me through the painful editing process. Your honest feedback and unconditional love humbled me. Thank you for being part of my tribe and teaching me divine kindness through your modeling. I love you with all my heart and am eternally grateful for you. Speaking of angels, special thanks to my work daughters, Caro Martinez and Cristy Sánchez. You make my life better! Thank you for your love, initiative, and unconditional support. I am grateful to have you and am excited to continue witnessing your growth and success. You are the secret to mine. You know what they say, " Behind every successful woman, there are Caro and Cristy." I adore you.

Sarah Cherres, I cannot thank you enough for helping me publish this book. I felt so lost before I met you. You have been patient, accommodating, kind, and so dedicated. It is because of you that I was able to meet my deadline to fulfill my dream of making this Fofi's birthday present for what would've been her 10th birthday. Thank you for your encouragement, your editing work, and your ever-present disposition to help. I know you worked really hard to make it happen and I want you to know that your efforts didn't go unnoticed. I appreciate you. Thank you so much for everything!

McKenna Martinez and Jessika Soto, thank you for helping me with the book cover with such patience and grace. After so many changes, I'm sure my readers would agree that it came out beautiful! I am grateful for you and pray God helps you in all your endeavors.

A big hug to all of you who have one way or another inspired me to write this book or supported me through the process. TheBetter with Betsy Team, my clients, the Hurt2Hope community, my social media audience, my friends, you...THANK YOU.

Finally, I have my favorite people to thank: my family. Mami, Papi, Suegris, thank you for your unwavering love and support. I am blessed to have you four as my parents. Thank you for teaching me about faith. I don't know what would be of my life if you hadn't planted the love for Jesus in my heart. Thank you for the babysitting, the encouragement, and for giving me all of my siblings. Having them in times of adversity made the difference. I love you forever.

Chichi, Gordi, and Mia, thank you for giving up so much of your time with me to allow me to write. I know I spent countless hours in front of the computer, when I would have wanted to be with you, but because of your generosity, you will be helping a lot of people through this book. I love you with all my heart and hope to always model for you the things I teach here.

Chichi, you are my favorite artist. Thank you for helping me design the book cover. Your creativity amazes me and your kindness moves me. I love that you've been on my team and that you've made my writing process so pleasant. You have a gift for making people feel special. Thank you for always asking how I was doing with the progress of the book and for celebrating every accomplishment. I am so grateful for your support, mi amor.

Alain, I had to leave the best for last. I could write a whole book on why I'm grateful for you, but I'll do it how you like it: straight to the point. THANK YOU. Thank you for helping me write this book by being a part of my story. You are my love, my partner, and my best friend. Thank you for letting me pursue my dreams, even when they take so much time away from you and our shared responsibilities.

Thank you for never-ever complaining about anything. Thank you for cooking, doing the dishes, providing for our family, attending to the kids, and still finding time to prepare my morning tea and every meal of the day. Thank you for getting me off my "writing chair" to go for a walk and rest my eyes. Thank you for listening to me rant and for making me laugh daily. Thank you for loving me without conditions or expectations. Thank you for making me the happiest woman on earth. I love you like crazy...for real...forever!

About the Author

Dr. Betsy Guerra was born in Puerto Rico and is the third of four siblings. Her parents are devoted Catholics who instilled the importance of spiritual and academic education in her upbringing. Leading by example, her mom and dad taught her about faith and service.

Betsy completed her doctorate in clinical psychology at the University of Puerto Rico in 2006. She then married the man of her dreams, Alain Guerra. Their fairytale was complete when they became the parents of Victoria (Chichi), Verónica (Fofi), and Gabriel (Gordi). They brought immense joy to their family and lived happily ever after.

ABOUT THE AUTHOR

Until...Tragedy knocked at their door. Fofi died before their eyes in a pool accident. She was two years, eight months, and 22 days old. Betsy's life was turned upside down. Her fairytale vanished. The pain consumed her. She didn't think it was possible to live without her daughter.

Remembering her parents' legacy, she turned to her faith. Betsy chose to believe—in God, in the process, and in the possibility that she could be happy again. As she pursued healing, she exercised her faith and clinical skills relentlessly. Her efforts led Betsy to joy.

During this process, Betsy was blessed with her fourth child, Mia. She then chose to devote her career to honoring Fofi through service. Combining her personal experience with her spiritual and clinical backgrounds, Betsy created a powerful approach to transforming hurt into hope. She teaches her clients and audiences how to navigate through their pain, strengthen their relationships, and develop the tools that will elevate their lives.

Contact

BetterWithBetsy.com
Hurt2Hope.com
IG and FB @BetterWithBetsy
LinkedIn Dr. Betsy Guerra
betsy@betterwithbetsy.com

Because independent writers and publishers should be held to the same high standards as the mainstream publishing industry, I encourage you to post an honest review of this book on Amazon.com, Goodreads.com or the online bookstore of your choice.

Thank you,
Dr. Betsy Guerra

Made in the USA
Columbia, SC
19 December 2020